Improvising Blues Piano

by Martan Mann
Unlock the mystery of blues improvisation as you develop an understanding
of different blues styles and express yourself through your music.
Contains scores of exercises specially designed to get you playing the blues right away.

Cover photography: SuperStock
Back cover photography: Trini Contreras

This book Copyright © 1997 by Amsco Publications,
A Division of Music Sales Corporation, New York

Order No. AM 945142

ISBN 978-0-8256-1624-2

Music Sales America

DISTRIBUTED BY

HAL•LEONARD®
CORPORATION
7777 W. BLUEMOUND RD. P.O. BOX 13819 MILWAUKEE, WI 53213

CD Track Listing

Contents

Acknowledgments

I want to wish a special thank you to the fine people at Music Sales Corporation: Barrie Edwards, Peter Pickow, Ed Lozano, Steven Wilson, Joey Lyons, Dave McCumiskey, Dan Earley, *et al*. I also want to thank many family and friends who were of invaluable support to me, especially my wonderful children: Candiya, Bhroam and Aaron. And, thank you to my eagle-eyed editors: Lynda DeRemer and Marilyn Johnson. I want to wish a special thank you to Margarita Zuniga for her support.

The compact disk was recorded direct to DAT at Jazzical Recordings in Aptos, California. Michael Jordan was the fantastic recording engineer. Michael Abowd, a digital wizard, performed the computer editing on Digidesign Pro Tools.

A very special thanks and appreciation goes to my good friends, musicians: Bob Blankenship, Charmaigne Scott, Donald Scott, Dr. Lewis Keiser, Mo Isaac, Frank Leal, and Stuart Zimney. Friends like these make life worth living.

Photograph of Martan Mann by Russ Fischella

Foreword

Welcome to the world of blues piano, a world of pure emotion. Don't bring your intellect here. Just let it all "hang out." Get into it. It's time to wail. Has life been good to you? Then celebrate. Has it been tough? Then commiserate. Above all, express yourself. And when you've finished playing…you'll feel better.

Now having said all that…we have quite a bit of work to do. After all, blues is a style of music, with its own theory, technique, form, attitude, and stylistic elements. There are scales to learn, chords to master, styles to be aware of and techniques to develop. Then you should be able to put all these pieces together to start playing the blues, both solo and in a group.

It is my philosophy of teaching that we learn an improvisatory activity by careful preparation of the subconscious mind. Simply learning about an activity does not give you the ability to perform it. One of my favorite methods of learning is similar to the methods developed by *Sybervision*. In this method, you train the subconscious by watching experts perform specific activities over and over. In studying the blues, we listen to great blues players and imitate their style and "licks."

This book is designed to help train you to play the blues. It discusses many styles and stylistic elements of blues. It does not just give you a few prepared tunes to play, or pre-designed "licks," tricks, or "one-size-fits-all" scales. Rather, it is a book that gives you the means to develop you as a blues player. I've accomplished this by giving you exercises. As boring as it may seem, practicing exercises over and over, allows the subconscious to transform obscure knowledge into easy, secure, effortless knowledge. If you practice step by step, the rest will be easy. When you begin to improvise the blues, you will automatically draw upon your newly aquired storehouse of knowledge in the subconscious. This is the fastest and most efficient way to become an expert in any musical style.

There are a number of musical elements to learn in the development of the blues style. You will need to know:

- **History of the style:** You need to know a little about where the blues came from. What were its influences? What directions has it taken? What music has it influenced? Who are some of its principle performers? What are some of its specific styles? Why is it played?

- **Basic Theory:** It is vitally important to know the "basics." What basic background theory do you need? For example: you need to play in all keys; you need to thoroughly know the "cycle of keys"; you need to easily relate to intervals. Mastering theory helps you develop your "ears." This is information that helps you to perform "without thought." Also, what are some of the theoretical elements which specifically relate to the blues? What is the blues form? How can you learn to alter or substitute chords? What scales and modes are used for soloing?

- **Playing skills:** How do you assimilate the necessary scales, chords, "licks" *etc.*? What kind of a "touches" do you use? How do you phrase? What kind of dynamics do you use? What about pedaling? How do you get the blues "sound?" How can you establish the correct "groove?" How do you learn to "comp?" How do you develop left hand, right hand independence skills? How do you learn to solo? How can you develop a piano arrangement? What progressions do you need to practice? How do you develop the blues "groove?" What is the difference between solo and group piano playing? How do you develop your "ears?"

- **Styles:** What are some of the main blues styles for the piano? What are their elements? Who played them? What do you listen for? How do you develop those styles? What kind of theory and piano techniques do you need to master for a specific style?

- **Listening techniques:** How do you transcribe licks and chords? Where do you go to listen to blues? What should you listen for? What is good blues?

This book gives you the means to develop yourself into a fully functioning blues player. This book and CD (and your own listening to blues players and recordings) will give you essential information: theory, advice, and written arrangements. The main key in style-training is to assimilate many elements into an emotional activity. The left brain starts with the specific elements and eventually the right brain assembles those elements into a musical and emotional whole. In other words, our goal is to play and enjoy the blues, not to think about it. There will be a necessary period of practice, but with diligent study, and careful listening you should be able, in a short period of time, to enjoy the emotional world of blues.

How to Study This Book

In Chapter One, some very basic theory is presented. Know this theory thoroughly. If you do not, spend some valuable time and completely assimilate all of it. It will be a shortcut to becoming a fine blues pianist.

This book is compiled around some generalized blues styles. As you progress through the styles, you will notice that the theory becomes more complex. Enjoy each style and simultaneously study the CD included in with this book. Work with the particular style and theory presented in that chapter, until you begin to see some results. Then continue on in the book and CD.

Develop freedom in expression. Practice all the exercises, chord changes, and musical examples. Remember to practice playing in all keys. Develop yourself thoroughly in all the blues styles. Play solo, develop your own piano arrangements, play in a group. Accompany a blues singer if you can.

Additionally, this book gives you some basic blues progressions enabling you to experience rhythmic groove, a good blues feel and right hand soloing techniques. As you continue studying the blues, you will find many variational forms with chord substitutions.

Each progression will contain instruction in the following areas:
1. Style
2. Form
3. Scales
4. Chords
5. Accompaniment patterns
6. Soloing patterns (licks)
7. Practicing suggestions

Because blues players cannot live by just the blues scale, and also because blues styles have "advanced" into jazz areas, this book provides some advanced study in Chapters Eight (Jazz Blues) and Nine (Minor Blues). The be-bop players in the fifties and sixties took blues into many different musical venues. In these chapters you have some harmonic devices which will take you beyond the common blues scale, such as: the II, V, I progression; the diminished scale and color chords; the melodic minor scale, other blues progression, *etc.* These have been given to you to pique your curiosity and to help you to creatively develop yourself beyond the usual blues scale. You should use these chapters when you are ready to expand your blues playing into different harmonic areas.

During this study, listen intently to the blues. Go out to blues clubs. Listen to recordings. Listen to all styles of blues. Talk with blues musicians. You have to surround yourself with blues to really appreciate it and develop yourself into a first-rate blues musician.

How to Study the CD

Listen to the CD, correlating it with the pages in the book. A "CD Track List" is included enabling you to find examples in the book that you have heard on the CD. (Note that the CD does not include all of the examples in the book. Those of which are on the disk are noted with a "CD" in the book.)

In my private teaching, I request that the student bring a cassette tape to the lesson. This has proved to be a most valuable learning tool because it allows the student to hear, feel, and analyze the examples, over and over if necessary. This is especially important when studying the blues where "feeling" is so important. Therefore, I have included a CD with this book.

Listen carefully to each style-section of the disk while looking at its corresponding chapter. In some cases the book will show you a close approximation of the blues phrases and voicings that are being played.

There are some sections of the tunes performed on the disk, where there is space for you to solo. If there isn't "space" to solo, feel free to play on top of what I am playing. Give yourself an idea of what it feels like to play the various blues styles. Use this device to learn other styles. Play a recording of a blues band and write down the chord changes. Then play along with the recording.

Musicians Heard on the CD

To add a dash of realism to this CD, I asked some musician friends to join me to play on this CD.

Boogie Woogie Blues:
> Charmaigne Scott, Vocals
> Donald Scott, Bass
> Bob Blankenship, Drums
> Martan Mann, Piano

Gospel Blues:
> Charmaigne Scott, Vocals
> Donald Scott, Bass
> Bob Blankenship, Drums
> Martan Mann, Piano and organ (really a Kurzweil K1000)

Stride Blues as performed by my Dixieland-Swing group, The Jazzical 6:

Dr. Lewis Keiser, Cornet
Frank Leal, Clarinet
Mo Isaac, Trombone
Stuart Zimney, Bass
Bob Blankenship, Drums
Martan Mann, Piano

Minor Blues:

Frank Leal, Sax
Stuart Zimney, Bass
Bob Blankenship, Drums
Martan Mann, Piano

This recording is a special remembrance of a wonderful friend and trombonist, Mo Isaac, who passed away last year.

How to Develop the Blues Styles

See the chapter on boogie woogie for a good example of learning any blues style. Here is a review of the learning steps:

1. Master the theory and technique examples given in each chapter until you can play them without thought. This starts with Basic Theory, Chapter One.

2. Master the blues forms by playing accompaniment patterns over and over in the left hand. First learn a set of blues chord changes so that you can play them "in your sleep." Even if it is with just a single note in the bass, it will help you to learn the style. Accompaniment patterns will be given to help you get started. It is through the repetition of these chord changes that you will develop the blues feeling that is essential in being a good blues player. Different chord progressions and chord voicings are given for each style.

3. Play the accompaniment in the left hand and the rhythmical comping chords in the right hand.

4. Play simple single bass notes in the left hand and melody and/or soloing in the right hand. (Study the stylistic soloing licks given in this book and CD, and listen to other recordings.)

5. Play comping chords on the left hand and soloing on the right hand.

6. Then, (the most difficult step) play a walking bass pattern with the left hand while soloing with the right hand.

7. Start making up your own solo arrangements by including all of the above steps. Play them for others.

8. Then, (the most important step) join in and play with other blues players and singers.

9. Continually learn new scales, chords, voicings, "licks," blues forms, *etc.*.

There is a video series which accompanies my books, entitled, *The Music Improv Series*. Please write the publisher of this book, Music Sales Corporation, for more details, or for information on how to contact me directly.

Good Luck, have fun!

Chapter 1
Basic Theory

OK, here it is...hold your nose, take your castor oil, learn your basic theory.

This chapter contains the most basic, fundamental music theory that you need to master...before studying the blues. Without mastering these "basics," your study of specific blues will be more difficult. Conversely, if you take the time to diligently assimilate this information, you will quickly be able to develop the various blues styles.

At the same time it is recommended that you begin developing your basic piano techniques. It is strongly suggested that you practice your major scales, minor scales, blues scales, diminished scales, whole-tone scales, *etc*. Also start working on arpeggios in triads and sevenths.

To develop your fingers, start playing "Hanon" exercises in all keys. I also highly recommend studying, *Rational Principles of Pianoforte Technique* by Alfred Cortot.

The point is, start now in preparing yourself to play the blues. When the opportunity comes to "sit in" on a blues jam session, you want to be ready.

The Cycle of Keys

The cycle of keys, also known as the circle (or cycle) of fifths (or cycle of fourths, *etc*.), is absolutely essential in the study of jazz and blues improvisation. The aspiring blues musician should endeavor to literally know this cycle backwards and forwards, inside and out. Blues players constantly relate to this cycle and use it to memorize tunes in all keys, create chord substitutions, and relate other jazz theories to it. As we continue on in this study you should use the cycle to practice technical and theory exercises. And as mentioned before, when you start learning blues changes, you will find this cycle of keys invaluable. (See example 1–1)

You can travel either direction around the cycle. If you move the direction of the flats, you are moving up four notes in the major scale. For instance, if your starting note is a "C," then you will count up four scale tones, i.e.: C, D, E, F. "F" starts the next key. Then continue around the cycle until you end back at "C." You will notice that at the bottom of the page, there are alternative routes, depending if you are traveling around the flats or sharps. These are called enharmonic keys. The *enharmonic* keys represent two spellings of the same scales played on the piano. For instance, C♯ and D♭ are the same note, but their scales have different spellings. You choose one or the other depending on the direction that you are moving around the cycle.

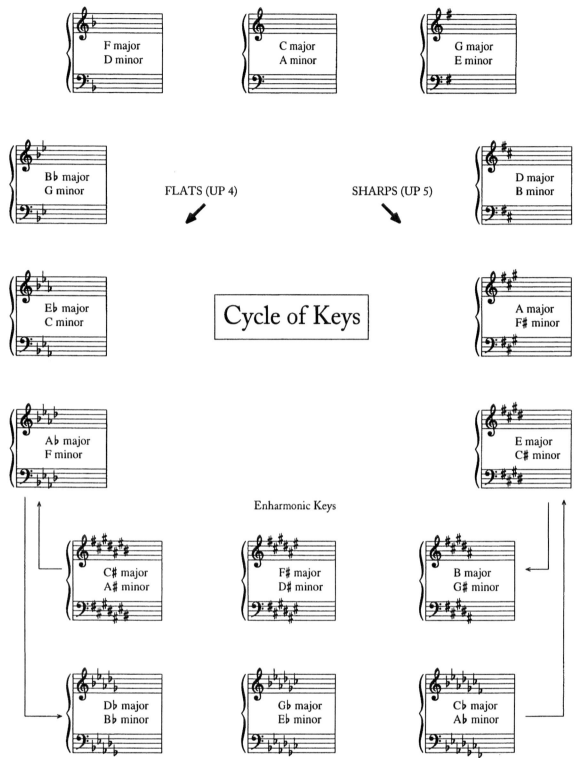

Example 1-1

Cycle of Keys Exercise

1. Start at the lowest "C" on the piano and begin moving up the keyboard playing up four diatonic (scale) notes around the cycle of fourths (flat direction). Remember you count up four notes, counting the first and last note, of the major scale. Therefore, you will be playing C, F, Bb, Eb, Ab, *etc.* Keep going until you return to "C." (see example 1-2)

2. Again start at the lowest "C" on the piano and start moving five scale tones up the keyboard playing around the cycle of fifths (sharp direction). This time you are moving up the keyboard counting five notes up the major scale. For instance, your bottom note is "C," then count up C, D, E, F, G. Then begin on "G" and count up five notes of the G major scale to "D" *etc.* Continue all the way around until you return to "C."

3. Now you will note that if you start on a "C" and move up four diatonic notes to "F," you could have also moved five diatonic notes down to "F." Similarly, if you move five notes up from "C" to "G," you can also move four notes down to a "G." So you can now practice arbitrarily changing directions as you move your way around the cycle. For instance, you might move up four notes from "C" to "F," and then down five notes to "B♭," and continue around the cycle arbitrarily changing directions on the keyboard.

Example 1-2: Cycle of keys exercise

Intervals

This section on intervals represents some very basic and important study. Sing the intervals, play them, repeat them from another player. This is "nitty-gritty" theory study. It is the basis for all improvisation and definitely the basis for playing in all keys. It needs constant work until you are well conversant with all of the intervals. (See example 1-3)

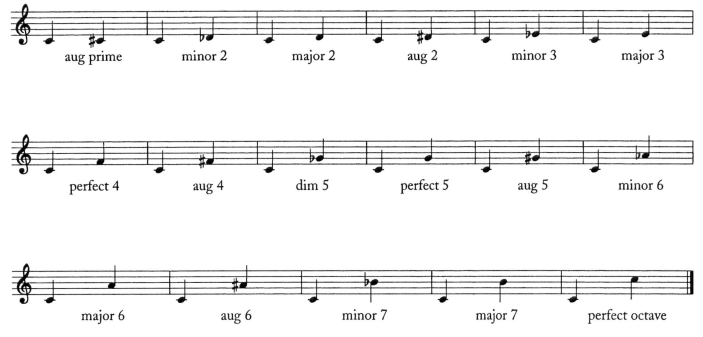

Example 1-3: chromatic intervals

Think Before Moving Exercise

Here is a good exercise to help you learn intervals. (CD) This is also a good way to learn all of your theory, since it develops quick thinking on the keyboard. This will greatly help your ability as an improviser.

Pick one interval, let's say a major second. Place your fingers on a major second, let your fingers rest there. (Play a major second.) Now arbitrarily visualize another major second. Do not move your hand until you firmly visualize the second major second. When you do, play the first major second and immediately, quickly skip to the second. When you have landed on the new major second, use this as a platform to make another jump.

When you are good at visualizing one jump, expand your thinking to two jumps. You can expand to three jumps or four. The main point is to visualize before moving. Move quickly to the new interval. Do not "hover" over the new position while trying to think where you are going.

Major Scales

It is recommended that you thoroughly master your major scales. Practice them first hands-separately and then hands-together. Play them in different meters, for instance, groups of twos and threes.

Play scales in different intervals between the hands such as thirds or tenths, fourths, seconds, *etc.* Play scales in random fashion so that you move spontaneously from one to the other at any time. This develops the improvisational ability to think ahead and develops good fingering practices for improvisation. Remember, when you are improvising, you do not have the opportunity to study and learn fingerings. They must be done mentally as you play. Dive right in and start learning these scales today. It's going to take some time to do. Be persistent.

Flats

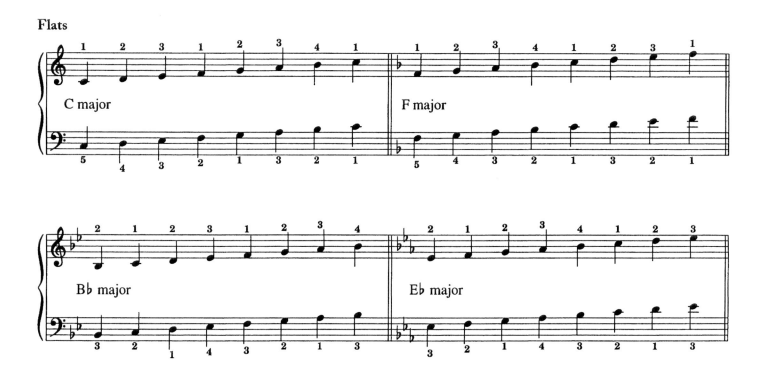

Sharps

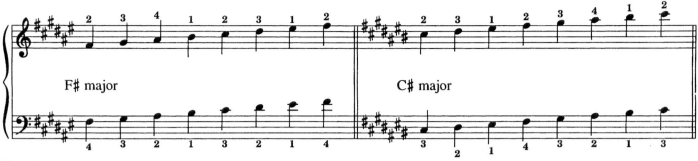

Example 1-4: major scales

Minor Scales

Once the major scales are learned, it is easier to learn the minors and the modes. Although the minor scales aren't usually thought of as blues-type of scales, they are, none-the-less, used in minor blues (and also the major blues). Remember, the minor third is a "blue" note. Incidentally, the Dorian mode is included because it is very similar in sound to a minor scale. It is recommended that you study the changes in the top tetrachord of the scale. That is where the subtle changes in the minors take place. (See example 1-5)

Example 1-5: major, minor and Dorian scales

Modes

The modes are a very simple concept to understand. Simply take a scale, in this case, major, and play it from each note to note in the scale: for example 1- 1, or 2-2. See the modes in order of degrees of the major scale. (See example 1-6)

Major Scale Modes
(in order of the degrees of the major scale)

degrees of the scale	mode	characteristics
1-1	Ionian	(same as the major scale)
2-2	Dorian	flat 3 and 7 (sounds minor)
3-3	Phrygian	flat 2, 3, 6, and 7 (sounds minor with flatted 2nd)
4-4	Lydian	sharp 4 (sounds major with sharped 4)
5-5	Mixolydian	flat 7 (dominant 7th)
6-6	Aeolian	flat 3, 6, and 7 (same as relative minor scale)
7-7	Locrian	flat 2, 3, 5, 6, and 7 (half diminished)

example 1-6

Learning the Modes

To learn the modes, it is recommended that you learn them by improvising on them one at a time. Also learn them from the same starting note, for instance "C." (See example 1-7) Now play first the Ionian mode from C-C or 1-1. Now raise the fourth and play the Lydian mode starting on "C." This is also 4-4 in the G major scale. Do not try, however, to refer in your mind to the G major scale—because the listener does not hear G major.

Next play the major scale with a ♭7 which is the Mixolydian mode. This mode works well with dominant seventh chords, such as in the blues. Now add a ♭3 to the ♭7 and play the Dorian mode, or 2-2 in the scale. Add an A♭ or ♭6th to the ♭3 and ♭7 and call that the Aeolian mode or natural minor scale. Continue on by adding the ♭2nd to the ♭3, ♭6, ♭7 and that is called the Phrygian. Lastly add a ♭5th to the ♭2, ♭3, ♭6, ♭7 and play the Locrian mode. Change keys often.

As mentioned before, the principle mode used in the blues is the Mixolydian mode. However it is still important to know, for instance, the minor-type modes, such as the Dorian, Aeolian, and Phrygian because they are, from time to time, used in the standard blues and certainly the minor blues. The Locrian mode contains the ♭5th and is often used in the more jazz oriented styles of blues. The Locrian is also used to solo over the m7♭5 chord.

When you are improvising, a chord change is immediately interpreted by the blues/jazz player as a scale or mode. For instance, the Ionian mode is used to play over the maj7 chords; the Mixolydian mode is used to play over dominant 7 chords; and the Dorian mode is often used to play over the m7. Then the player develops his improv from those tonalities.

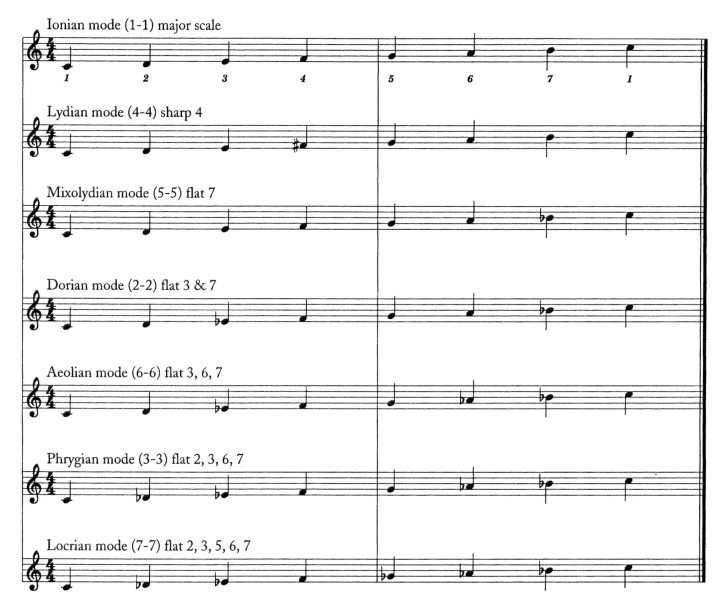

Example 1-7: Major scale modes (with the same starting note)(The order of modes has been re-arranged)

Triads

It is very basic to learn all the triads…and also all the sevenths, in all of their inversions (in all keys). Practice all the chords as solid chords and also as arpeggios (broken chords). Even though the dominant seventh (with the ♭7 degree) is the basic chord for the blues, the other sevenths often come into play. A good blues player uses a variety of chords. Study the chords in closed and open voicings. (See examples 1-8 through 1-14)

Analyze the chords and their inversions by visualizing the intervals which construct the chord. For instance the major triad is constructed with a major third on the bottom and a minor third on the top. The minor triad is the reverse, a minor third on the bottom and a major third on the top. (See example 1-8) Study all the triads, sevenths and inversions in this manner.

Incidentally, the diminished triad was not listed in inversions because it is a more complete chord as a diminished seventh. (See example 1-12)

Example 1-8: all triads and inversions

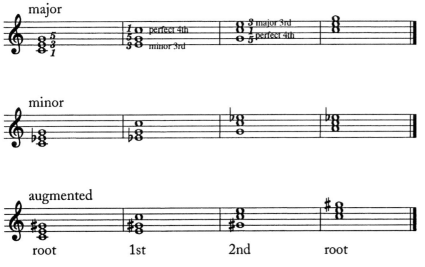

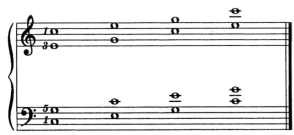

Example 1-9: triad inversions

Open Voicings

We create an open voicing by moving the third of a chord up an octave. (See examples 1-10 and 1-11) This spreads the chord between the hands. Try the same exercise with all the sevenths. This is also the beginning of developing good voicing for the blues. This is especially useful in playing the gospel blues style.

Example 1-10: open voicings in inversions

Example 1-11: additional open voicings

Note the broken dividing lines in the above example group the open voicings according to the left hand interval. This has been provided as a study help.

Sevenths

Get to know each of these sevenths. Play them in all keys. Play them in all inversions, in arpeggios. Notice that they are grouped according to the triad on the bottom. Therefore, when hearing the seventh (the sixths are also included), first hear the base triad, then listen for the coloristic seventh. Play the "Think Before Moving" exercise to learn all the sevenths. (See example 1-12)

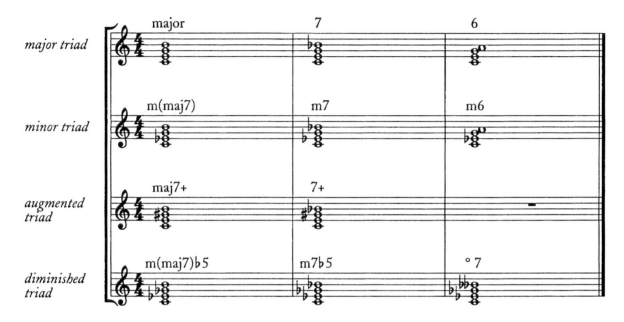

Example 1-12: seventh chords

This is a way to play your scales in sevenths. Play in all keys. Notice that the type of seventh changes as you move up the scale. This is a good way to learn all of your scales.

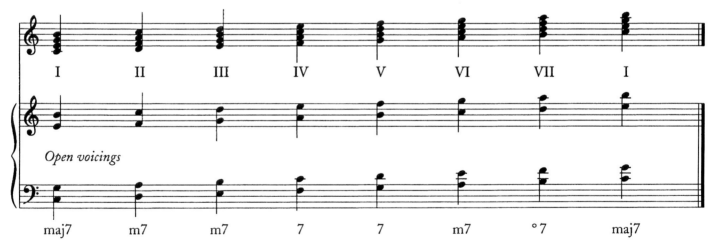

Example 1-13: major scale sevenths

Here is a series of major sevenths. Notice that the first chord is in the root position, which alternates with the next chord in the second inversion. Play the appropriate root in the left hand. Once you have mastered the major sevenths, then learn all of the sevenths in this manner. (Up 4, down 5, as in example 1-6)

Series of major sevenths

Example 1-14: series of major sevenths

Chapter 2
The Boogie Woogie Blues Style

The Basic Blues

The blues is really two different things, a style and a form. The blues style is instantly recognizable because it usually portrays the picture of hard times. It has been portrayed by many vocalists, such as Billie Holiday, B.B. King, Ray Charles, and Aretha Franklin, and numerous jazz pianists, trumpet players and guitar players, *etc*. When sung, the songs often tell of troubled relationships and problems. There is a lot of honest feeling in the blues. Often, not always, the blues is played slowly, with sliding notes (blues notes) and short, terse phrases. Blues can also be played in a hard driving, happy, upbeat style. Blues is prevalent in styles from Dixieland, to swing, to bebop, to today's current rock, fusion, country, and contemporary jazz. There are many, many recorded examples of good blues styles. Also, it is strongly recommended that you go to a blues club often and hear live blues to familiarize yourself with this style of music.

The Blues Form(s)

The blues form relates to a specific set of chord changes over which blues players like to improvise. The patterns are very universal and are literally known to all blues players. The most popular blues form is the twelve-bar blues. (CD) (See example 2-2) However, eight-bar and sixteen-bar blues are also common. There are many chord variations on this form and once you have mastered the basic forms, it is easy to learn substitute chord progressions.

The basic twelve-bar blues progression should be studied as three groups of four measures. The first group describes the I chord area the next group describes the IV chord area (two measures of IV and two, of I; and the final four measures actually describe the V chord, which accomplishes a "turnaround"). The *turnaround* is the ending progression which takes you back to the top (beginning) of the tune. The turnaround will be more fully discussed later in this book.

The Boogie Woogie Style

The boogie woogie style dates back to the early 1900s, and is distinguished by the left hand ostinato or repeated pattern. There are many boogie woogie left hand patterns. In the 1910-1930 era, there were many pianists who made their reputation primarily playing the boogie woogie, such as Gene Ammons, Pine Top Smith and Jelly Roll Morton. The boogie woogie pattern that I have chosen for beginning study is simply one of many. Some additional boogie woogie left hand accompaniment patterns will be given later in this section. (See example 2-12)

Groove Tune

There are several reasons why I have chosen boogie woogie to begin the blues improvisation of this book. This boogie woogie pattern constitutes what I term as a "groove tune." (CD) A groove tune is a tune, or more precisely, a chord progression which is played over and over. Usually the left hand is repeated over and over while the right hand "comps" or solos. This accomplishes several things. First, it gives you something to play as a solo pianist which sounds complete. This is important because many blues pianists today only play with groups and as a result do not feel comfortable playing solo. It is important to first be a good solo pianist, because then you have a command over all the elements of the music: melody, rhythm, and harmony. Then when you add other instruments, they are augmenting your mastery of the parameters of the tune that you are playing. All of the pianists of this boogie woogie era were fundamentally solo pianists.

Secondly, it requires that you, and only you establish the rhythmic groove. This groove is a term which is usually foreign to the non-jazz player. The term refers to the rhythmic feeling generated by a jazz tune. Remember the phrase, "It don't mean a thing if it ain't got that swing?" This refers to the subliminal message established by the groove. Some jazz players spend more of their energies establishing the groove than others, but all are conscious of it as a major part of the blues style. Even in a rubato ballad, groove plays an important part of the style.

When you find yourself tapping your foot or snapping your fingers (in blues, always on beats two and four), you are aware of the groove. A blues player often tries to make the groove better or "deeper" as the tune progresses through the choruses. If you play the boogie woogie over and over, eventually you will relax with the pattern until the groove becomes automatic. Then you will notice that your rhythm loosens up as your subconscious takes on more of the duties of controlling the rhythm. At this point you will probably feel the urge to take more liberties with the boogie woogie improvisation. However you must still keep the chord pattern consistent.

Listen to players who are considered good groove players, such as Oscar Peterson, Monty Alexander, Ahmad Jamal, Ray Charles, Dr. John, *etc.* Actually, any good blues player can be considered a groove player. Also, listen to the big bands, such as Count Basie's.

Developing the Boogie Woogie Style

1. Play the Boogie Woogie example 2-6, with both hands and with a $^{12}_{8}$ feel (a quarter note followed by an eighth) until you can play totally with ease and you begin to feel the groove. Strive for a good boogie woogie groove. You do not want a break when you shift from chord to chord. If you play this enough, your conscious mind will stop controlling the activity and the subconscious mind will take over. You know that you have established a good groove when, after you have stopped, you can still feel the groove in your body and emotions. Imagine, for fun, that you hear 20,000 people all clapping to your groove (on beats two and four, of course). (CD)

Example 2-1: twelve-eight feel of Boogie Woogie

2. Next, continue with just the left hand as you have been playing and start playing rhythmic chord figures in the right hand. You can use the examples in this book to get you started, and then add in your own. Again, listen to recordings for more ideas. It is vitally important that you start to think rhythmically. Rhythm and rhythmic figures form the foundation of your soloing. (CD) (See examples 2-7 and 2-8)

3. Practice soloing with the right hand, first without the left hand boogie woogie pattern (to establish phrasing), (See example 2-14) playing only a single root note in the bass, and then later with the boogie woogie accompaniment. (See example 2-12) The reason for this is to free up the right hand's phrasing from being locked into the boogie woogie accompaniment.

The Blues Scale

The *blues scale*, which you have probably heard or read about, is a scale which originally developed naturally out of the feelings of the blues players. In the early days of the blues, the players simply followed the styles of the day from their ear. Today, we are more prone to study and analyze the blues styles and thus have developed the term, blues scale as one of the principle means for achieving the blues sound. (See examples 2-4)

I mention this because I believe that the blues scale is generally over-stressed and over-used. Today's young rock and jazz players often learn this scale and then let their fingers run wildly up and down the scale without giving much thought to the melodies that they are making. The result is a boring, uncontrolled improvisation.

You will immediately notice that the fingerings of the six-note blues scale is awkward, especially if played over a two octave span. (See example 2-5) The chart on page 28 shows one set of fingerings for the right hand. There are other ways to finger these scales and you are encouraged to seek them out, especially if you do not like the examples given.

Practice all twelve while playing a single root note in the bass or you can use a simple dominant seventh consisting of root, third, flat seventh, or just the third and flat seventh (tritone). Play the fingerings over a two-octave range. Play the scale in every way imaginable. Then change keys until all twelve are comfortable. This scale is a good starting point for your blues improvisation and is especially helpful when learning the blues in all keys.

The Mixolydian+ Mode

Although, I use the blues scale often, I recommend a slightly different perspective on its use. Instead of thinking of the blues scale as a specific scale, work off of the Mixolydian+ mode (which contains the ♭7) and liberally add in ♭3rds and ♭5ths. I have coined the term, Mixolydian+ mode for this scale concept. The ♭3rds, ♭5ths, and ♭7ths can be called blues notes. The difference is that now you have a better chance to create melodies, much in the same way that the original blues singers and instrumentalists created their blues songs and melodies. (CD) (See example 2-3)

Actually, rather than just learning scales, I suggest listening to blues records and imitating the licks (melodic sequences), trying to maintain the style and inflections. The licks are usually not too difficult to hear and reproduce. Try singing them first, then playing them. (CD) Then place them in your improvisation notebook. Notice the extensive use of repetitive sequences. (There is a nifty little cassette recorder, by Marantz, which plays music back in half speed. This makes it easier to hear the licks).

Play licks over the pattern (in all keys) until all the blues scales are totally comfortable. Then progress to practice all of the blues styles using this scale as a starting point. Again and again, I want to emphasize that this scale is only a starting point in your improvisation. As said before, think of creating good melodic ideas. Develop good continuity from idea to idea. Tell a story. Be dramatic. Create excitement.

Example 2-2: Mixolydian (with added ♭3 and ♭5)

Example 2-3: blues scale

Example 2-4: blues scale fingerings

Important Soloing Ideas

1. Master the blues scale and the Mixolydian+ mode (with the added ♭3rd and ♭5th). (CD) (See examples 2-2, 2-3, 2-4) Master the blues form(s) that you are going to use for soloing. (See example 2-5) Master the accompaniment pattern that you are going to play in the left hand. You really can not begin to solo until you have total control of the above.

2. Listen, listen, listen to great blues players and singers!!!

   Many players have tried and tried to play written jazz solos, only to find that the written solos do not end up sounding like blues. I think that the main problems in playing written solos are in not knowing the original rhythm, touch and phrasing. Also, in playing written solos, the groove is non-existent. For instance, the correct groove in the boogie woogie blues is a $^{12}_{8}$ feel. But that $^{12}_{8}$ is not totally precise and must be learned through listening to blues players. It is a dialect in the language of music.

   A better way to learn blues is to learn specific licks from a recording, then transfer them to your notebook. Now play it on the piano while singing the phrase the way it was originally played or sung. As suggested before, this time do not play the left hand boogie woogie pattern, but rather, play one note in "stop time." Stop time is a term which means that the drummer or the band accents the first beat (or another beat) and the rhythm stops. The soloist solos over this empty space. Then the band punches in on the next first beat, *etc.* This allows you to hear the basic root tone and solo with looser phrasing.

   Put special emphasis on the rhythms that the right hand melodies make. In other words, listen to, for instance, a blues band and clap one of their melodic rhythms. Then go over to the piano and play that one rhythm over and over, making up different melodies from the Mixolydian+ mode or blues scale. Take special care to play the rhythmic phrasing exactly as the band plays it. You will find that you can create many melodies from that one rhythm. (See example 2-10)

   For instance, take one rhythm and play through an entire blues pattern just using only that rhythm and altering the melodies. Change the scales or modes with the chord change, i.e.: Use C Mixolydian+ or C blues with the C7; F Mixolydian+ or F blues with the F7, *etc. Note:* It is also possible to use the C Mixolydian+ or the C blues scale over all the chord changes throughout the blues pattern. Don't forget to add the $^{12}_{8}$ feel throughout. (See example 2-14) The "feel" and phrasing is vitally important to playing the blues.

   Listen extensively to great jazz singers like Sarah Vaughan, Ella Fitzgerald, Nancy Wilson, Mel Torme and Frank Sinatra, to name just a few. Also, listen to guitar, trumpet, or sax players to hear how they float over the groove. Mastering this concept and feel is essential to developing a good jazz sound.

   Listen, especially to drummers. Groove like a drummer and you will begin to sound like a blues player. Good drummers have a wonderful sense of rhythmic phrasing. They also think about the groove constantly while they are playing a tune. And, if you are fortunate enough to play with a good drummer, he/she will feed you many ideas to play. Always try to fit in with his phrasing when you are comping.

   Listening to this book's CD will help you to feel the boogie woogie groove. On the CD, there are many sections where I am playing the blues patterns over and over. This is a good opportunity for you to practice your right hand soloing. Just feel free to solo over the rhythm that I am playing. From time to time, I suggest that you record your soloing for your own critical analysis.

3. Another problem which you will be immediately confronting is perfecting hand independence. The left hand pattern must be learned so well that you can literally play any melody, in any time frame, against it. Of course, the left hand must be establishing the groove and the right hand plays the part of a vocalist or instrumentalist. The soloist (right hand) should be free to not have to lay down the groove. He can float over the groove, making melody. This is very difficult to master because the tendency is to play time with the soloing hand. Then, everything locks in and the blues sounds clunky and unnatural.

Remember the hands do not always come down precisely together. If you listen to a jazz vocalist or instrumental soloist, you will not hear them playing in total sync with the rhythm section. There is a natural sense of rubato to their phrasing. You should first establish the rhythm-section groove, then add in the free-floating feel of a soloist (your right hand).

A suggestion is that you try practicing rubato, putting all the emphasis on the phrasing of the solo. At this point, do not worry about the groove. Then after you have developed this, add in the left hand boogie woogie pattern, trying to maintain the same phrasing in the right hand. This is very difficult, but if you persevere, eventually your subconscious will learn this new language.

4. Many young jazz and blues students have concentrated on learning jazz and blues scales and modes…without studying melodic rhythms and phrasing, only to find that their solos sound like run-on sentences instead of well-crafted solos. A solo should have a beginning, a middle, and an end. It should "say something." The melodic ideas should follow good melodic principles of tension and release. There should be sequential and idea development. Also the melodic ideas should always resolve purposefully and cleanly. Then the phrasing will make sense and the ideas will have power.

5. Practice some sample endings. (See example 2-11) Actually they are variations on a theme. There are many endings which can be used.

Have fun, this is just the beginning! Start now by immersing yourself in the world of blues.

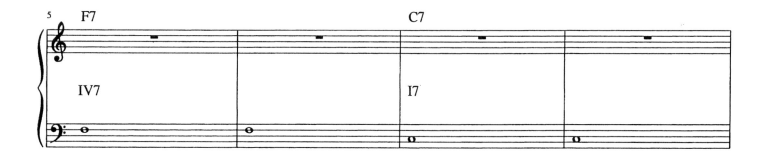

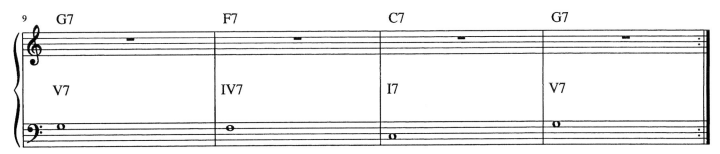

Example 2-5: basic twelve-bar blues progression

(Play in a **12/8** feel)

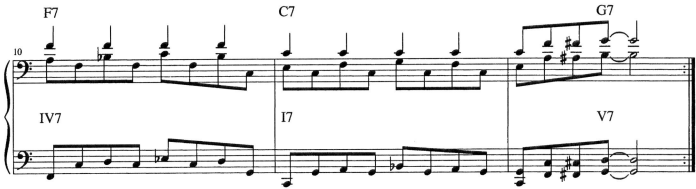

Example 2-6: basic boogie woogie blues

(Play in a **12/8** feel)

Example 2-7: boogie woogie with rhythmic patterns #1

(Play in a **¹²⁄₈** feel)

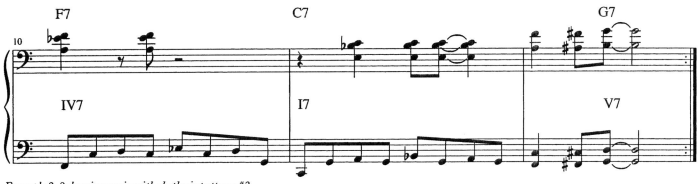

Example 2-8: boogie woogie with rhythmic patterns #2

(Play in a **12/8** feel)

Example 2-9: boogie woogie blues lick

It is popular in boogie woogie soloing to alternate in the right hand melody between the thumb and the other fingers. (CD) (See example 2-9) Actually, in my personal teaching, I usually do not teach by having the student copy my favorite blues licks, because this does not encourage the student to improvise on his/her own. Also, I would rather that the student make a practice of listening to a wide range of blues and jazz musicians of different instruments to develop new discoveries. The student, ultimately, is encouraged to develop his/her own style based upon extensive listening and playing. It is important for the student to try to compose tunes and licks and chord progressions, *etc.* Blues is a music of self-discovery. Having said that…I have included some blues ideas to help give you are start. Also, listen to the CD. (CD)

A good way to formulate licks in a particular style is to first recognize the fundamental rhythms that are used for most of them. I call them "melodic rhythms."

As an exercise, clap out the rhythms below. Then, using the blues scale(s), formulate many licks. Of course, it is recommended that you listen to blues recordings, and follow the process of first listening to the melodic rhythm, then recognizing the actual notes played. Don't forget that these rhythms are played with a "swing" feeling. Hear the drummer in your head.

(Play in a $\frac{12}{8}$ feel)

Boogie woogie licks based on the rhythmic licks above

Example 2-10: rhythmic lick ideas

(Play in a $\frac{12}{8}$ feel)

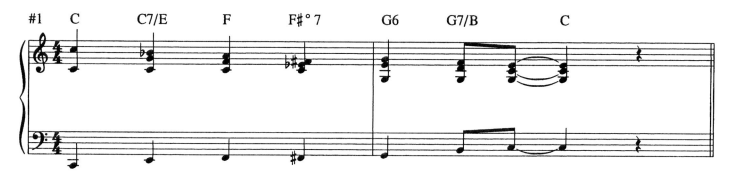

Example 2-11: sample endings

This is a partial sampling of boogie woogie basses. Usually boogie woogie is written in $\frac{4}{4}$ time with the $\frac{12}{8}$ feeling being understood. For the purposes of clarity, I have written them in $\frac{12}{8}$. Play these basses in all keys and practice the blues scale, the Mixolydian mode, and your blues soloing over it.

Example 2-12: some boogie woogie basses

Example 2-13: soloing melody to one note

Example 2-14: soloing using repeating ideas

CD Performance of Boogie Woogie Blues

On the recording, superb singer, Charmaigne Scott, Donald Scott on bass, Bob Blankenship on drums, and yours truly on piano, perform a "down and dirty" basic boogie woogie blues. Keep in mind that this recording session was very spontaneous—unrehearsed. This allowed for a great deal of interaction between the musicians. Also, it lead to some inspired changes from the textbook analysis. Why not! These performances on the CD are designed to add an element of fun and musical realism to this book. They are not meant to be copied exactly. However, they are an excellent source to hear, feel, and analyze the blues in action. Feel free to join in on our session. Jump right in.

There are several elements to this performance that I would like to mention for your analysis:

1. There was a slight variation from the basic blues progression given before. Notice that the IV7 (F7) chord is utilized in measure 2 for harmonic interest. On the first chorus that Charmaigne sings, the piano plays II-V-I (D7♭9, G7) leading to the C7 in measures 7 and 10. That II-V-I also came up in the ending chords (this time with a Gsus4 chord). (See example 2-15)

2. Although there are a few times where the piano and voice play a pure blues scale, most often the notes are selected with a melodic sense. This comes back to the idea of the Mixolydian+ mode with the added ♭3rd and ♭5th. When you are comping or soloing, you are reacting to the moment, trying to maintain continuity with what was played before. Often, the pianist fills in the spaces left by the soloist. I was not thinking of playing examples of the blues scale, or any specific licks. I was thinking melodically, rhythmically, and harmonically in an expressive and musical manner.

It is an important concept that the melodic ideas often move from one chord to another. In other words, the ideas resolve. You do not just play up and down the proper scale. Additionally, notice the use of space. I did not throw in idea after idea, or just let my fingers run wild. Allow time to think. At the ending, you can hear the effect of stopping the music. The space created a special tension.

3. Notice the groove. It is interesting that when we first decided to do a basic blues, I was thinking of a faster tempo and quite a different groove. But when we first started playing it, the groove wanted to fall into that slower rather funky, groove. That was fine with all of us. The main challenge then, was to maintain that groove throughout the performance. The main challenge for you, as you play the boogie woogie too, is to first become aware of the groove, copy it, then maintain it.

4. There are a few licks that I have written out for you. (See examples 2-16) If you are trying to learn them, notice the timing, phrasing, touch and dynamics of the way they were played. Quite often the right hand plays melody with closed position three-note chords. See if you can learn some of my licks off the CD.

5. There were several boogie woogie basses that I used. There wasn't any particular reason for using one or the other. My mind was on the emotion of the moment.

6. Just in general, notice the use of rhythmic syncopation. This helped the groove and created more excitement. Also notice the special effects, such as the *glissandi* (fancy word for quickly sliding your fingernails up the keyboard). Incidentally, don't overdo effects.

7. Pay particular attention to Charmaigne's use of lyrics and the way she uses them to sing jazz phrases. Blues has special meaning when sung. Lyrics tell a story. Lyrics convey special emotion. Notice her phrasing, dynamics, rhythm, *etc.* This is particularly important because pianists do not often consider the phrasing of lyrics when performing. Notice that the piano in the recording often leaves space for the vocalist to sing, then answers with a lick or comping.

Now, master the blues form below (See example 2-15) and start playing your own performance.

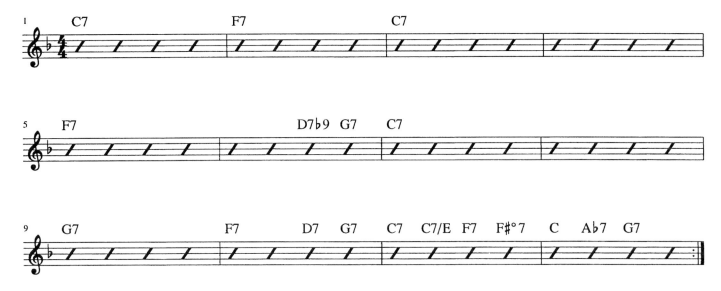

Example 2-15: boogie woogie blues chord changes

1)

Example 2-16: Blues licks

End of the last four bars of the first piano chorus

Measure 3, 2nd vocal chorus

Measure 4, piano solo chorus

Measure 10, piano solo chorus

Chapter 3
Tritone Blues Style

The Tritone Blues Style

Here is a blues groove tune which features a repeated quarter note figure in the left hand as the rhythmic ostinato. The figure utilizes the 3rd and ♭7th of the dominant chord. This interval, a ♭5th, is also known by the term *tritone*. When we delve later into the subject of substitute harmony, you will find many references to this interval. For now we will familiarize ourselves with this interval through playing it in this blues progression.

This style is often used by guitarists who softly comp in a "chunk-chunk-chunk-chunk" rhythmic pattern behind soloists. Listen to early recordings of the Nat King Cole trio or Freddie Green's guitar style in Count Basie's band.

This style is presented, not primarily for its importance as a blues style, but because it is an excellent learning device. It helps you to develop hand independence, to develop the blues form, and to develop soloing. This also becomes an introduction to chord substitutions.

The Tritone Blues Form

Notice that the chord pattern is a variation from the basic twelve-bar blues that we used for the boogie woogie blues. (See example 3-1) As we progress through the styles, the blues chord patterns will change. These changes usually represent good basic information regarding chord substitutions in general. In blues, you will hear many variations of these substitutions. When you listen to a blues recording, try to pick out the chord changes, including the substitutions.

Here are some of the harmonic adaptations used in the tritone blues:

1. In measure 2, the F7 or IV chord substitutes for the I chord. This is a common substitution for a "stagnant" I chord.

2. In measures 7, 8, 9, and 10, a I-IV-II-V turnaround is substituted for the standard chord changes. This leads smoothly to the I chord in measure 11.

3. A brief mention should be made about the use of a common jazz harmonic idea, that of playing a chord ½ step above or ½ step below as a lead-in to a chord. Chromatic chordal movement is very common in jazz. For now, when improvising over the chromatic chords, use the Mixolydian+ mode.

Development of the Tritone Blues

It is recommended that you start playing the pattern with a simple root note played by the left hand and the repeating tritone in the right hand. Play over and over until completely comfortable. (CD) (See example 3-2)

Then play the tritone with the left hand and play rhythmic figures with the right hand, as you did with the boogie woogie. Experiment with different rhythmic patterns. (CD) (See example 3-3)

Now add in some simple right hand soloing figures while playing the quarter note, tritone ostinato in the left hand. (example 3-5) For comping practice, try using the right hand rhythmic figures in example 3-3 in the left hand. Then solo with the right hand. It is difficult to keep the left hand figure going during soloing. It requires excellent hand independence. (CD)

Theory for the Tritone Blues

Continue to use the blues scale and the Mixolydian+ mode that I recommended for the boogie woogie blues. (See examples 2-3 and 2-4)

Incidentally, regarding the chords which are not I, IV, and V, such as the A7, should be played for now mainly with the Mixolydian+ mode. Later, you will use other scales such as the diminished scale over these chords. But, for now you can develop many melodies using the Mixolydian+ mode.

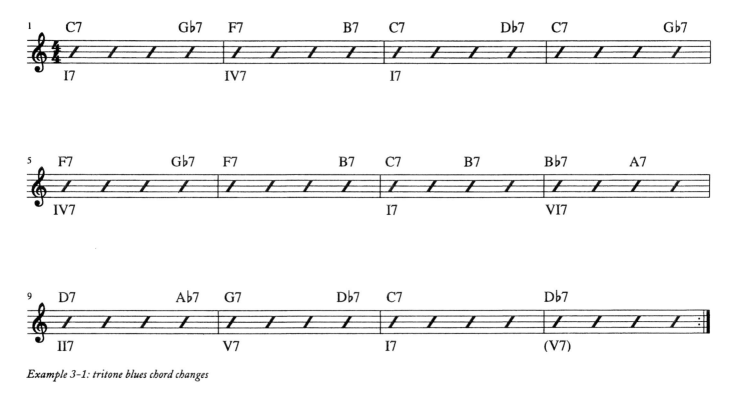

Example 3-1: tritone blues chord changes

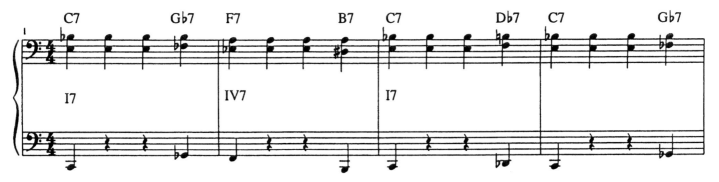

Example 3-2: tritone blues (left hand bass, right hand ostinato)

Example 3-3: tritone blues (tritone in left hand, rhythmic figures in right hand)

ezample 3–4: tritone blues (single note in the left hand, soloing in the right hand

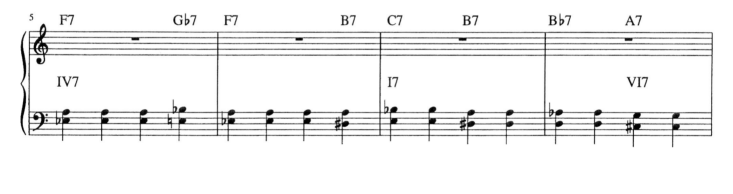

example 3-5: tritone blues (tritone in left hand, soloing in the right hand)

Chord Extensions

If you have ever looked at a jazz fakebook, you will have noticed chords adorned with extra numbers such as 9ths, 11ths and 13ths. These *extensions*, counting up from the root, add additional color to the triads and 7ths. Also, in the common practice of leaving out the root when playing extensions, they also add the element of ambiguity which is essential to using jazz substitutions. There are some mental tricks, however, that you can learn which will make it easier to master these extensions. The chart below lists the common extensions and their equivalents, one octave lower. (See example 3-6)

It is vitally important that you develop a facile working relationship with these extensions if you want to play jazz and blues. It will probably take a great deal of perseverance and diligent practice to master the extensions, but it is well worth it.

♭9th	=	m2nd
9th	=	2nd
♯9th	=	m3rd
11th	=	P4th
♯11th	=	Tritone (Aug.4th)
♭13th	=	♭6th (Aug.5th)
13th	=	6th

Example 3-6: extension equivalents

Extension Exercise

How to Learn Extensions

The best way to learn extensions is to first play and recognize the 3rd and ♭7th (tritone). You must designate a root tone in your mind (you do not have to play the root). It is relatively easy to spot the 3rd and ♭7th (tritone) in a dominant chord. A dominant chord is created from the Mixolydian mode, which is a major scale with a ♭7th.

A commonly played chord using the Mixolydian mode is the 9/13 chord. This chord has the 3rd, ♭7th, 9th and 13th (remember, the 9th is one octave higher than the 2nd and the 13th is one octave higher than the 6th). This chord often plays from V to I. (See example 3-7)

For the purpose of this chapter, we are going to use the 9/13 extension which easily applies to the blues which we have been playing. To ease into the use of extensions, let's start with something that we already know. Take the tritone blues and add two additional extension notes to the tritone. (See examples 3-8 and 3-9) Note that we are adding a 9th and a 13th. Now explore the blues, this time using the 9/13 chord extensions in the left hand. Use the Mixolydian mode and blues scales to improvise over these chords. This is a good opportunity to start to play in other keys, eventually all keys.

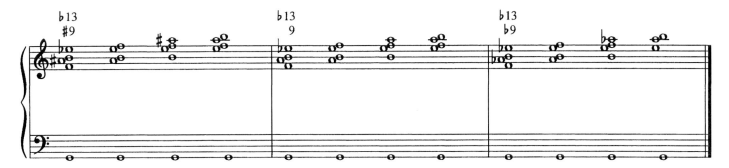

example 3-7: commonly played dominant extensions

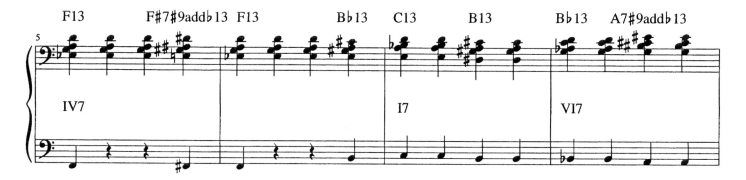

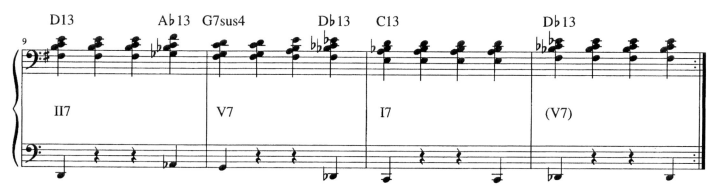

example 3-8: tritone blues (using extensions in right hand, single notes in left hand)

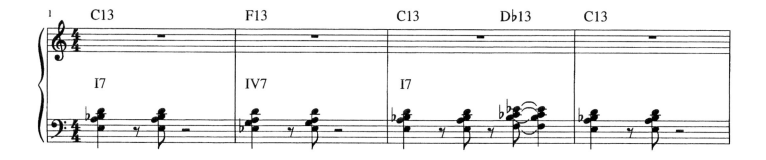

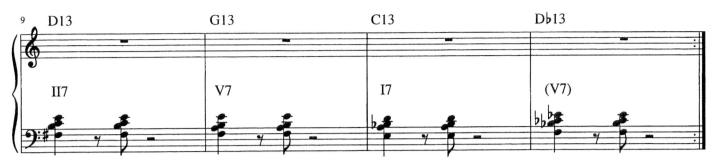

Example 3-9: tritone blues with extensions (comping left hand, right hand soloing)

Continuous Motion Exercise

Try the continuous motion exercise to develop continuity in your soloing. Start playing a continuous, spontaneous melody with even quarter notes. Just play them continuously, trying to make musical sense as you go. You want your ideas to come out logically. This causes you to think while you are playing. Then do this exercise in eighth notes, eighth-note triplets, and sixteenth notes. Then vary between the different time values. Finally, develop the use of space in your melodies. (See example 3-10)

Use the Mixolydian mode, the Mixolydian+ scale, and the blues scale. You may also use chromatic approach notes. The main point is to play continuous ideas which are musical to your ears.

Of course, this is an exercise and I don't recommend that you play this way in your actual blues soloing.

Example 3-10: continuous motion exercise sample bass for soloing

Chapter 4
Gospel Blues Style

Hallelujah! It's time to play some feel-good, soul-lifting, happy-time gospel blues. The roots of this type of blues probably is in the early hymns. Look for lots of Amens (that's IV to I). As a pianist (or organist), if you want to plumb the depth of your blues feelings, experience backing a great gospel blues singer like Charmaigne Scott. As with the performance of the boogie woogie blues, you are hearing the true inspiration of our initial communication (along with Donald Scott on bass and Bob Blankenship on drums) on "Amazing Grace." (CD)

In general, this is a good time to review all of your beginning triad progressions. Look at the I-V7-I, I-IV-I, I-IV-V7-I progressions in both closed and open voicings. (CD) (See examples 4-6 and 4-7) You will see a predominance of triads. Sometimes the triads are played in transition with the 3rd in the bass. Also look for ♭7ths (dominants). In addition, this is a good time to check out the diminished triad, °7th chord, and diminished scale since you will find a number of diminished chords used primarily in transitions.

Look at the "Chord Structures Exercise," especially playing the Mixolydian+ mode. This can be very helpful in both comping and soloing. (CD) (See examples 4-8, 4-9 and 1-10) Take a scale, the Mixolydian+ mode, or blues scale, for example, and play melodies using chord structures from that scale. The more that you practice this, the better you will become.

Development of the Gospel Blues Style

1. To develop the gospel blues style: first practice playing the I-IV-I and I-V-I progressions in closed and open voicings. (See examples 4-6 and 4-7)

2. Secondly, practice playing chord structures. Chord structures allow you to create chords out of scales. For instance, take the Mixolydian Mode. (See example 4-8)

3. Create a shape in your hand. Then play up and down the Mixolydian mode in that structure. (See example 4-9) Do this with many different structures. Then you should be able to mix and match different structures out of the mode. Now play melodies harmonized only by structures out of the Mixolydian mode. For blues purposes, add in the ♭3rd and ♭5th.

4. Notice the form of the gospel blues style as presented in this book. You will observe the use of °7ths as passing chords. Also notice the use of the 3rd of the chord in the bass. Also observe the II-V-I in measure 14. These harmonic elements help to form the gospel blues style. (See example 4-1)

Analysis of "Amazing Grace" CD Performance

Many jazz players have the mistaken impression that the blues must be in a twelve-bar form. The true blues takes many forms and expressions. In this case, classify the sixteen-bar "Amazing Grace" as a blues original. Also, please note that this hymn is in ¾. (It also could have been written in ⁶⁄₈.) Notice the rolling triplet feel.

There are several attributes to the piano gospel blues style as presented in the performance of "Amazing Grace":

1. There is frequent use of octaves in the right hand.

2. The right hand often plays closed position chords with the left hand playing either an octave or single bass note. Observe the use of the 3rd of the chord in the bass.

3. The style is often basic and simple.

4. The style often is developed from the chordal style of church hymns.

5. The I, IV, and V chords predominate. Practice the Chord Structure Exercise (4-8, 4-9, and 4-10) and the I-IV-V-I progressions. (4-6 and 4-7)

6. The °7th chord is often used as a transition.

7. The Mixolydian mode and blues scale are most often used for melodies.

8. Listen to the gospel singers for phrasing, dynamics, and touch.

9. The accompanist often plays an "answer" after the vocalist has sung the "question."

10. Notice the use of arpeggiated chords, grace notes (actually, crushed notes in jazz), tremolo, and other effects.

11. Good advice: Go listen to a live gospel choir. Listen to the good groove. Clap your hands. Enjoy the great feeling.

Development of "Amazing Grace"

On the following page, I have included a written example of the piano accompaniment of the first chorus of "Amazing Grace" on the CD. Of course, this is not meant to be learned note for note, but to be used as a suggestion for your own gospel accompaniments and piano solos. Listen to the entire song and analyze the ideas. Find other recordings to listen to. This style is not difficult to develop and is a great way to dive into the blues.

For the purpose of teaching the gospel style, I have chosen the hymn, "Amazing Grace." Incidentally, "Amazing Grace" is not technically blues-it is a hymn. However, it contains all of the elements of blues and blues styles.

1. Study the "Amazing Grace" chord chart. (See example 4-1)

2. Play single note in the left bass and melody in the right hand. (See example 4-2)

3. Play a single note in the bass and a harmonized melody in the right hand. (See example 4-3)

4. Start playing the chords to "Amazing Grace" from the chord chart given in the book. (See example 4-4)

5. Finally mix all the elements into your own arrangement of "Amazing Grace." Track? shows you an approximation of the actual arrangement on the CD. (See example 4-5)

When listening to the CD performance of "Amazing Grace," listen for the use of octaves, I-IV-V progressions; the use of arpeggiated chords, crushed notes, tremolo, *etc*. If you want to play along, please do.

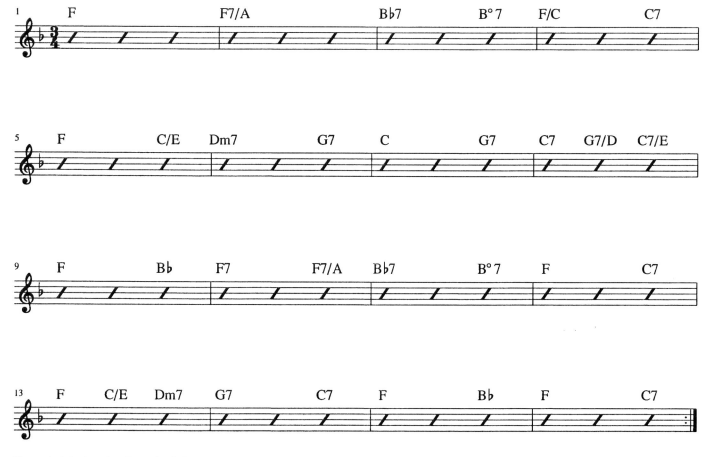

Example 4-1: Amazing Grace chord changes

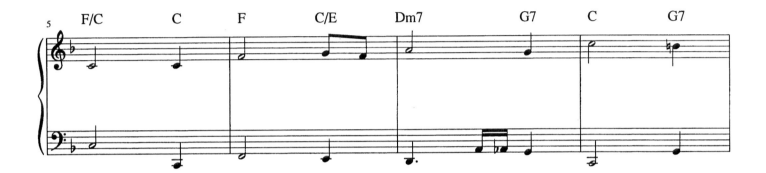

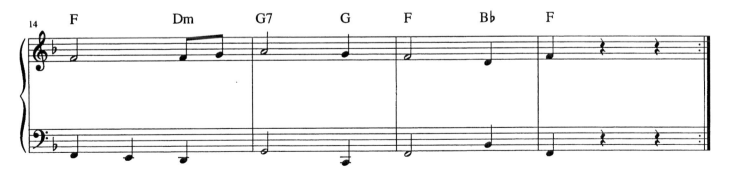

Example 4-2: Amazing Grace (single note in the bass, melody in right hand)

Example 4-3: Amazing Grace (single note in the bass, harmonized melody in right hand)

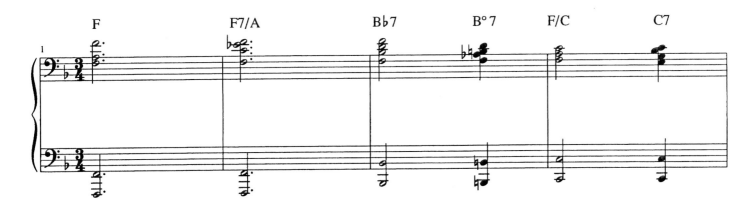

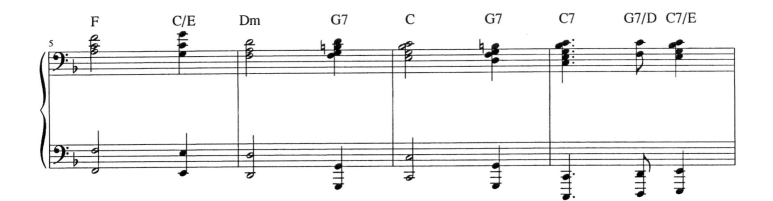

Example 4-4: Amazing Grace (playing basic chords from the chord chart from page 50)

Accompaniment to first vocal chorus

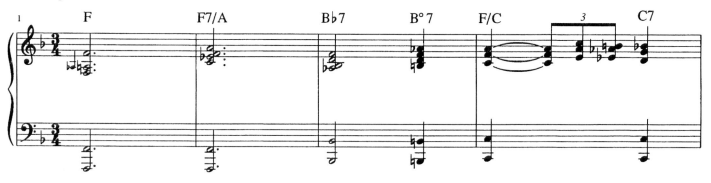

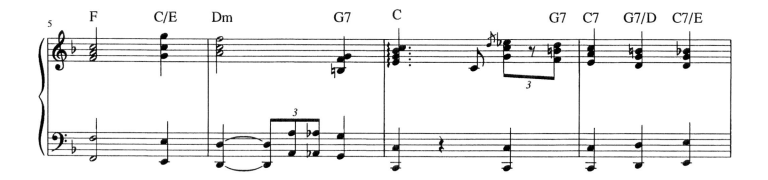

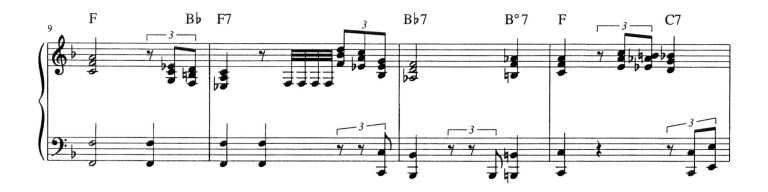

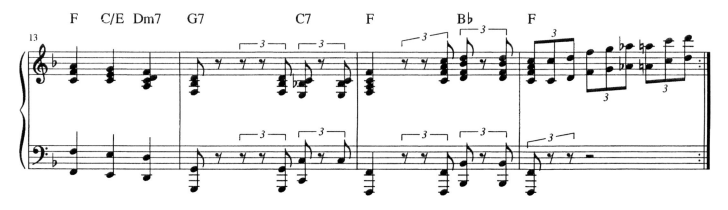

Example 4-5: Amazing Grace as played on the CD

Progressions

Practice playing from a major triad to a V7 chord, such as C to G7 and back to C. Also play I-IV-I; I-IV-I-V7-I; and I-IV-V7-I progressions. Play in inversions. Play in minor as Im-V7-Im; Im-IVm-Im; Im-IV-Im; Im-IVm-V7-Im; and Im-IV-V7-Im. Experiment with progressions around the cycle in fourths, fifths, or chromatically. This is especially a good tune-up to play a gospel blues style.

Example 4-6: closed voicings

Here are some progressions using the open voicings. These are based on the open voicings that you learned before. The best way to learn these is to start with a I chord, then experiment with the next chord. This is why it is called, "make up your own progression." Try to keep the voice-leading smooth, without large jumps. Remember: Do not double the third. Also try the progressions listed in the prior paragraph.

Example 4-7: open voicings progression

Chord Structures

One of my favorite ways to learn a new scale or mode, is to play the game, chord structures. Chord structures is deceptively simple. But I know first hand in my own experience as a player and a teacher that it works. This is a very good way to get to know any scale or mode inside out. I highly recommend practicing this with all scales that you want to learn.

We will start with the Mixolydian mode. Choose a structure, let's say fingers 1, 2, 5 in the right hand. If you hold that structure, you can play up and down the scale using 1,2, and 5. The intervals will slightly change as you move up the scale. Now comes the hard part, play this in all keys.

Practice this exercise in any structure of your choice. Make sure that you play in all keys. Next, break up the structures into arpeggiated figures. Play the structures in any order. (See example 4-8)

Lastly, play melodies using just the Mixolydian mode. At this point, you can mix and match the chord structures. (See example 4-10)

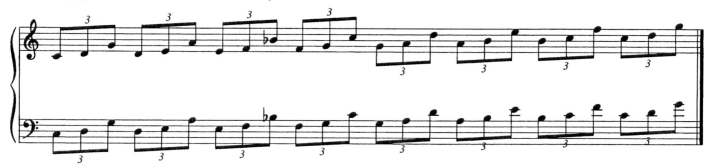

Example 4-8: chord structures

Example 4-9: chord structures in the second inversion

etc.

Example 4-10: melody with chord structures (mix and match the structures out of the Mixolydian mode)

Chapter 5
Stride Blues Style

Who says that the blues has to be sad? Listen to good Chicago or New Orleans Dixieland blues and often the music is jumping. Usually, the Dixieland style has a front line of trumpet or cornet, clarinet, and trombone. The rhythm section consists of a banjo and/or piano, bass or tuba, and drums (or washboard!) I used this style as a showcase for the stride piano style because the piano naturally falls into this style in performing its function in the group.

The stride blues style is not limited to Dixieland by any means. Many early pianists, such as Fats Waller, Art Tatum, and J.P. Johnson played the stride piano as a solo piano artform. Today, you can listen to Dick Hyman, Mike Lipskin, and Ralph Sutton, among others. This style was a mainstay for all early blues pianists. Like the boogie woogie, stride allows the piano to play a full solo piano style.

Fundamentally, the stride blues style consists of the left hand playing a swing or stride left hand against any right hand soloing. The bass accompaniment takes many hours (days and months) to master. Playing Scott Joplin's music is a great way to experience a very classy stride accompaniment. Also, there are many written arrangements by Fats Waller and others, where you can study and learn the stride accompaniment.

Here are some exercises to help develop this accompaniment style. In all cases, endeavor to practice the exercises in all keys. Practice the exercises first using two hands, (left hand on the bass note and right hand on the chord) then use only the left hand. If you wish and are able, you can improvise melodies with the right hand (start very slow). This is also a good practice with first learning a new tune or blues progression. A word of warning: If you haven't played a lot of stride, be careful of over-using the left hand. Sometimes, you can develop a muscle strain if you practice too much.

As with all styles, you must listen carefully to the stride blues style of others to develop it in your playing. Especially with playing Dixieland, the music is never written out (except the melody and chord changes). The pianist, as well as all the other musicians, just know what to play. This comes from listening to good bands, and analysing what the pianist is playing in different parts of the improvisation process. Listen to the chord changes, rhythmic timing, left hand accompaniment, right hand licks, *etc.*

In this section on stride, we are going to use the stride accompaniment to master some vital blues/jazz theory. In particular, this section will help you to master:

1. the triads and 7ths in all inversions;

2. the basic I-VI-II-V turnaround; and

3. the infamous tritone substitution

First there will be a discussion of the theory, followed by exercises performed by you in the stride blues style. All of this theory is used by both the early and later jazz pianists. The main difference is that today's pianists do not often use the stride accompaniment. More modern accompaniment will be covered in the section on "Jazz Blues."

Stride Triad and 7th Inversion

First and foremost, it is important that you practice the left hand alone until it is very quick, precise, and automatic. A good place to start is with a simple swing bass which has the left hand starting with a single bass note and then swinging up to a chord.

"Stride Exercise 1" has you alternating between root and 5th in the bass note with moving up triad inversions in the upper chord. You should also practice this exercise using all the triads and sevenths. Notice that this exercise also utilizes the I-IV and V keys centers. (See examples 5-1)

Play first with two hands, then with only the left hand

Example 5-1: stride exercise #1 inversion

The Turnaround

The turnaround, as its name implies, is the transition area of the tune which returns the tune back to the beginning of a section, or carries it on to the next section; for example, the "bridge." Very often, the intro can also be a turnaround and sometimes, the ending is a turnaround. If the turnaround repeats over and over, without a set place to stop, this is known as a "vamp." There are also many occurrences of the turnaround in blues.

A very common turnaround is the "Heart and Soul" or "We Want Cantor" vamp of I, VI, II, V. In its most natural form, within the key, it is written as I, VIm, IIm, and V7 dominant. (See examples 5-2 and 5-3) Stride exercise 2 uses the basic turnaround as a stride exercise. This is very important because in the original "barrel house" or stride blues style, this turnaround was constantly used. You must be proficient in the stride turnaround.

It is also fun to start improvising in the right hand over the I-VI-II-V chords, once you have gained proficiency in the stride left hand. You have two main choices of scales from which to solo. The first, (and not my favorite) is to play the major scale for all of the changes. Since all of the chords in the basic turnaround are found in the major scale, this will work. However, my personal choice, and one which causes subtle differences, is to play the Ionian mode for the I chord; the Dorian (or Aeolian) for the VI chord; Dorian for the II chord and Mixolydian for the V7 chord. Even though the notes are essentially the same, the way you treat the notes will be different if you play with the modes. (See 1-6 and 1-7 in Chapter 1)

Play in all keys

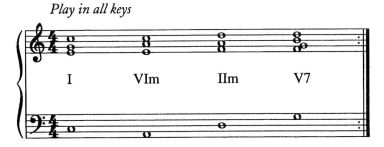

Example 5-2: original turnaround

Play first with two hands, then with only the left hand

Example 5-3: stride exercise #2 using the I-VI-II-V7 progression

Tritone Substitution

A tune can sound reasonably well with the standard changes, but in jazz and blues, it is universally accepted that you have license to substitute and alter the chords. The alteration of chords relates to the changing of the chord type, for instance from major to minor, or from a maj7th to a ♭7th. In doing so, we are also altering the scale that we are using for soloing. Chord alterations and different scales will be discussed in the section on "jazz blues style," but for now we will discuss chord substitutions, which means to substitute one chord for the original.

By far the most often used chord substitution in blues and jazz is the tritone substitution. Once you begin to master this substitution, you will start to understand much of what you hear in jazz and blues. This tritone substitution is used over and over. It is the foundation of most intros, turnarounds, and many endings of songs. It is a convenient way to modulate to a new key. And, it is a primary method of jazz soloing and comping. Bass players freely utilize this substitution.

To start, let's return to the blues and the tritone accompaniment. Remember, we played the 3rd and the ♭7th (tritone) as the primary intervals in the 7th chord. It is interesting that if you play a 3rd and ♭7th, let's say "B" and "F," the root is "G." Now if we exchange the root for a "D♭," which is a tritone away from "G," now the "B" and "F" are reversed. The "B" is the ♭7th and the "F" is the 3rd. (Note: "B" is the enharmonic equivalent of "C♭".) This is another way of pointing out that both "G" and "D♭" share two of the same notes (in reverse). (See examples 5-4 and 5-5)

This means that in many cases, not all, if you see a "G7" on the chart, you can substitute a "D♭7" for it. Keep in mind that this works for some styles of jazz. It usually does not work in other styles such as country western, pop, and rock. Also, a major determining factor of whether or not the tritone substitution will work, is the melody of the tune. Sometimes you have to change the melody to make it work, or simply not use that kind of substitution.

The examples which follow will give some variations which you will find as you use the tritone substitutions. For instance, in example 5-4 below, if the second chord is an "A," which is the 6th, it can be substituted by an "E♭," which is a tritone away. By doing this, you can have many combinations. Note the relationship of 4ths and also chromatic half steps. The I chord has been substituted by the III and it's tritone sub., the ♭VII. The III is the next chord around the cycle of keys. Therefore it is natural to use E, A, D, G, to C. (or III, VI, II, V, I).

In the first chart: "Variations of the Tritone Substitutions," you have the opportunity to quickly learn and hear the tritone substitutions. Practice these substitutions extensively, in all keys, until you can play and hear them automatically. (See example 5-4)

Then practice the same exercise using the stride accompaniment in stride exercise 3 (See example 5-5). It is also recommended that after you develop some proficiency in this exercise, that you begin soloing in the right hand. It is recommended that you use either the Mixolydian mode, the Mixolydian+ mode, or the blues scale.

1.

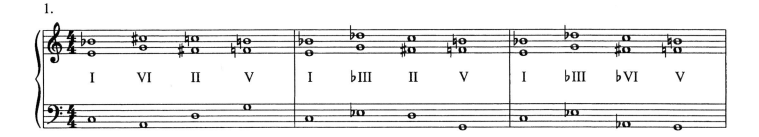

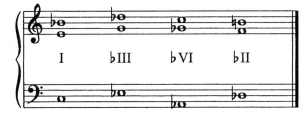

2.

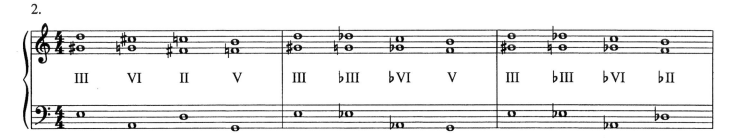

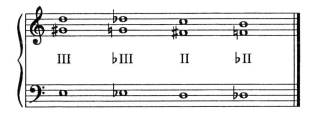

3.

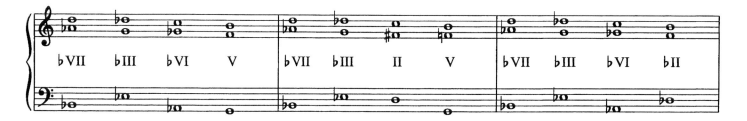

Example 5–4: variations of the tritone substitution

Stride exercise 3 shows many of the variations of the tritone substitution. If you listen to Art Tatum or Teddy Wilson recordings, you will hear many uses of the tritone substitutions.

Example 5-5: stride exercise #3 using the tritone substitution

Miscellaneous Stride Techniques

Stride exercise 4 gives you many different techniques used by stride pianists. (See example 5-6, below)

1. Uses 10ths. If you have trouble playing the tenth, consider quickly arpeggiating from the bottom note to the top note.

2. Uses 10ths and 6ths.

3. This is a good method if you have a small hand or if you are playing very rapidly.

4. Notice the octave passing tones.

5. 10ths and 7ths

6. Similar to 3 except that the tritone is played.

7. Combinations of 5ths and tritones. stride exercise 5 uses some combinations of rhythm changes. These changes, loosely derived from "I've got Rhythm," are found in many jazz tunes. (Play in all keys.)

Play first with two hands, then with only the left hand

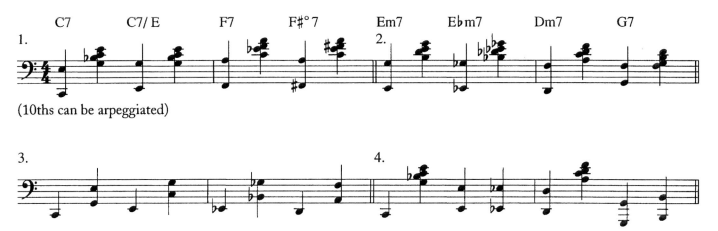

(10ths can be arpeggiated)

Example 5-6: stride exercise #4 miscellaneous stride techniques

Example 5-7: slow stride blues in G chord chart

Example 5-8: Bye and Bye chord chart

Stride exercise 5 follows the chord changes of the old tune, "Bye and Bye," played by the Dixieland band on the CD. The left hand pattern does not exactly follow the patterns that I played, but gives you ideas to develop. (See example 5-9)

Play first with two hands, then with only the left hand

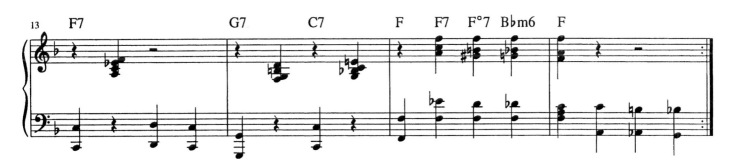

Example 5-9: stride exercise 5) Bye and Bye from CD performance

Chapter 6
Funk Blues Style

The funk blues style is typified by a highly syncopated and very rhythmical pulse. The feeling and the tempos are down and earthy. The syncopation is intensified by the use of rhythmical space. A good way to learn the funk style is to first listen to the funk rhythms of drummers. Start clapping funk rhythms on your knees. (Make sure to use kneepads for this exercise.) (See example 6-1)

Example 6-1: sample funk rhythm (clap on knees)

After that, turn your attention to the bass players to establish the left hand patterns. If you listen to the CD, you will hear many different rhythmical patterns. This becomes automatic after playing awhile.

Stop Choruses

In the recording, we will first explore an idea called stop choruses. This is a good way to learn to solo and also a good way to start to develop the funk blues style because it gives you room to phrase. The piano plays a chord or short lick. This is followed by a space of time where the soloist improvises. I am going to play some stop time choruses as a means for you to solo. I will be playing some of the soloing licks and then leave space for you. Feel free to solo or play your own funk accompaniment as I continue through the choruses.

Chord Structures

Secondly, we are going to develop the idea of chord structures. In chord structures, you are playing a scale as chords. This means that you can play 2, 3, 4, or more notes of a scale together as a chord. One way to practice this is to create a structure, *i.e.* 1, 2, 4, 5, and play that structure up the scale (in all keys). Then you can practice playing melodies and comping using different structures from various scales and modes. This is an excellent way to learn your scales. Notice in the written example the use of harmonizing the melodies in the right hand. (See example 6-2)

Use this CD performance as a general guide to playing funk rhythms and chord structures. Of course, listen to other recordings, and make up your own funk tunes and funk rhythms.

Developing the Funk Blues Style

1. The funk style is a more modern blues style. This style is very rhythmic and is generated primarily from the drummer and bass player. If you want to learn to play funk, start by listening to drummers, then play the rhythms with your hands. (See example 6-1)

2. Next transfer that rhythm to the keyboard by playing a single note in the bass and a chord in the right hand. For practice, you can just use one chord change for awhile until you have established the groove. (See example 6-2)

3. Then play lead-ins in the bass. Refer to the written tune in this chapter. To develop these lead-ins, listen to and copy funk bass players. Use chord structures in the right hand. Soloing in the funk style is difficult because you often have to keep the funk patterns going and finding time to put in melody solos is difficult. Basically, you have to work out of the rhythm. Therefore, it is suggested that you just play the rhythmic accompaniment until you start to become so comfortable that you can add in some soloing notes. (See example 6-3 and 6-4)

Example 6-2: funk rhythm with single note in bass and chord structures in right hand

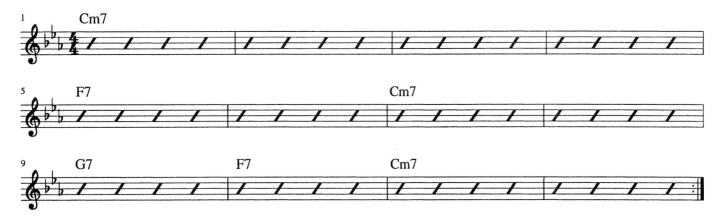

Example 6-3: funk style chord chart

By Martan Mann

Example 6–4: "Santa Cruz Funk" lead-ins in the bass

Chapter 7
Rock Blues Style

There are many rock styles. The best book that I have found on rock piano styles is *Improvising Rock Piano* by Jeffery Gutcheon. This book thoroughly discusses the rock piano styles, including blues rock. For those of you primarily interested in rock piano, I recommend that book. Here is one of my favorite rock styles. It is a style popularized by, among others, Jerry Lee Lewis. It is a derivative of the boogie woogie style except the groove is different. Notice the boogie woogie pattern is more even and that there is a small accent on the alternate eighth notes.

Start by playing this pattern in both hands, then play with just the left hand. Start slowly and pick up speed with practice. Stay loose, do not force. If you feel yourself tightening up, stop and relax. Of course, as with the other blues styles, try to find other musicians and vocalists to play with you. It really helps to establish the style.

Practice the "Blues Rock Accompaniment" performed on the CD until you can play it effortlessly at a fast tempo. Try to place the accent on the afterbeats as shown in the music. (See example 7-1) Then start listening to rock piano recordings. Find some favorite licks and write them down. (See example 7-2) Then practice them in all keys. I have provided some possible licks and endings. (See example 7-3)

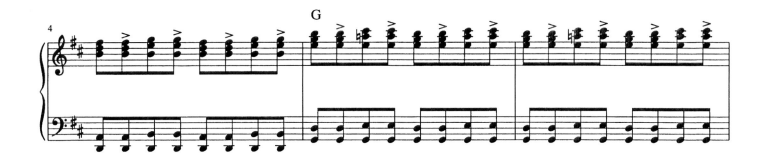

Example 7-1: blues rock accompaniment

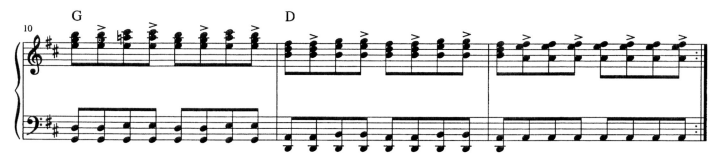

Example 7-2: some blues rock licks

1.

2.

3.

4.

Example 7-3: some blues rock endings

Chapter 8
Jazz Blues Style

The jazz blues style is really the subject for another book because the study of jazz is so complex and has become such an involved artform. For further study on jazz piano, I recommend my book on jazz study, *Jazz Improvisation for the Classical Pianist*. Actually, we could easily consider this chapter as advanced blues. This, and the following chapter, should give you some ideas for adding new harmonic concepts into your playing.

It isn't possible to teach this advanced blues style, without discussing advanced jazz theory. Therefore, this chapter will begin with the most important of this jazz blues theory. As with studying all theory for jazz improv, practice the exercises until they are effortless and easy for you. Once this theory is mastered, putting the pieces together into a jazz blues whole is relatively easy.

This chapter will take great deal of time and effort, and also additional jazz study to perfect. However, it will help you to understand the evolution of the blues and jazz. Here are the subjects which are covered in this chapter:

1. We will discuss the II-V-I progression. You must know this progression inside and out.

2. We will discuss the diminished chord and the diminished scale. This will help you to hear the progressive jazz sound of the bebop years.

3. We will discuss the creation and use of chord voicings. An idea is presented which will enable you to utilize any chord. You have to have a systematic method to first insert that chord or voicing into your subconscious and then find ways to spontaneously use that chord once it is available to you.

4. Some scales for jazz soloing will be presented. Remember, when you see a chord on a chord chart, that chord represents a soloing scale. Your soloing will be enhanced by learning new scales.

5. We will study a series of blues forms. There are many variations of the blues forms. These are just a start.

6. We will develop a jazz blues style through mastering a blues form and developing bass accompaniments for soloing. This requires many elements of mind and hand coordination. Listen to the CD for some helpful examples.

II-V-I Progression

This is the best single harmonic concept in developing a jazz blues playing style. Learn the II-V-I progression in all keys. Add extensions and chord alterations as you go along. There are some examples in this book. Mastering this concept will take some time, but it is certainly well worth it.

Practicing II-V-I

1. Develop a routine. Practice the II-V-I progression systematically: e.g., move around the cycle of fourths and fifths, then proceed up and down the keyboard chromatically. Use the IIm9 for the II chord, V13 for the V chord, and Imaj9 for the I chord. Visualize ahead while you play. Play with the chord in the right hand and the root in the left hand.

2. Then play the chords with the left hand and sing the root.

3. Then play with the chords in the right hand and a walking bass in the left hand. (CD)

4. Play the chords in the left hand and try improvising with the right hand. (CD)

5. Finally, if you are ready, play a walking bassline with the left hand and improvise with the right hand. (CD) (See example 8-5)

When improvising, use the Dorian mode for the II chord, the Mixolydian mode for the V, and the Ionian for the I chord. Also for blues practice, you can substitute the II9 or the II♭9 for the II chord and the I7 for the I chord. You can also play a I-VI-II-V progression with the above steps. (see example 8-4 and 8-5) (CD) In this case use the altered scale for improvising over the VI chord (See example 8-16)

Once you have developed the II-Vs as above, you can then alter the II-V-I as you experiment. (See example 8-6)

Flat Direction

Example 8-1: II V I progression in major (left hand single bass, right hand chords)

Sharp Direction

Example 8-2: II V I progression in major (left hand single bass note, right hand chords)

Example 8-3: II V I progression in major (only left hand chords)

IIm9   V13   Imaj 9   VI7#9addb13

Play chords in all inversions

Example 8-4: II-V-I-VI progression in major (left hand single bass note, right hand chords)

IIm9   V13   Imaj 9   VI7#9addb13

Make up your own walking bass. Play in all keys.

Example 8-5: II-V-I-VI progression in major (left hand walking bass lines, right hand chords or soloing

II Minor Chord

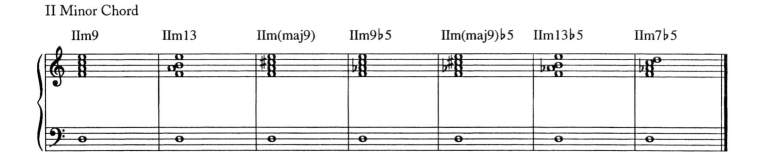

V Dominant Chord

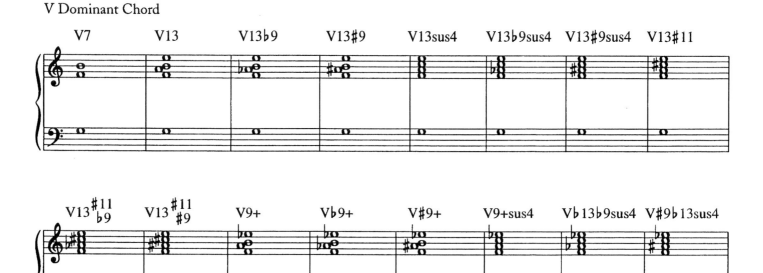

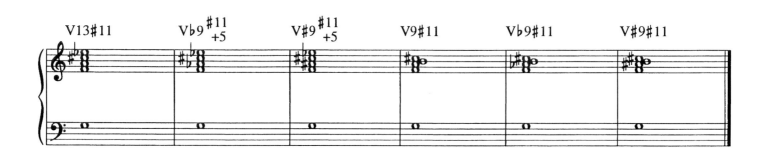

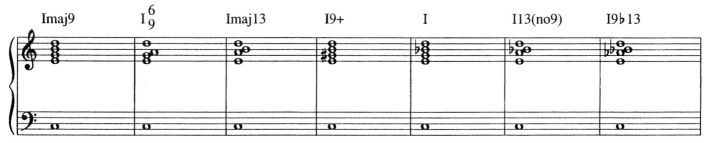

I Chord

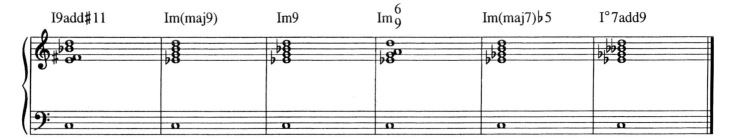

Example 8-6: some possible alterations of the II-V-I chords

Diminished Scale and Color Chords

Start learning all the diminished scales. Learn the whole-half and the half-whole diminished starting on every note. (See example 8-8) Practice using the diminished scale for soloing. It is primarily used for soloing over the dominant chords. Think of a whole-half diminished off of the ♭9th of the chord. Once you start using this scale, you will hear it being used by many jazz players. Practice the diminished exercises in this chapter.

Color chords provide an easy way to thoroughly learn your diminished harmonies. Mix and match all of the color families of dominant sevenths for some surprising sounds. (See example 8-10)

Remember, that in jazz soloing, as with the blues soloing presented before, that you should ideally be making melodies, not playing scales. Think of melodic phrases.

The diminished scale and color chords will instantly dress up your chords and melodic soloing. (See example 8-9) Also, given the nature of the diminished scale as an "equal distant scale," it is very easy to learn and hear. The diminished scale is built around the minor third intervals which make up the diminished seventh chord. These minor third intervals are equally proportioned from octave to octave. The scale can be constructed as a half-whole or a whole-half diminished. (See example 8-8)

The scales should be played with two hands until thoroughly known. The diminished scale is primarily used while playing either a dominant or diminished chord. In this case, the player thinks of a whole-half diminished scale off of the ♭9th of the dominant chord. (See example 8-9) Notice the extensions which fall into this scale and which extensions that do not. For instance, you can play the ♭9, and ♯9, but not the major 9th. The sharp 11 and 13th works but the flat 13th (sharp 5th) does not. The scale works very well with the diminished seventh chord. To be completely safe, you can just play the tritone 3 and flat 7 chord in the left hand. The sharp 11, flat 9 chord works well and also happens to be the tritone substitution dominant chord.

Color Chord Exercise

Color chords are a way of combining four dominant chords. (See example 8-10) The roots of these dominant sevenths are a minor third apart, which describes the notes of a °7th chord. When the notes of these dominants are combined, all the notes in a diminished scale are present. For instance, the combination of B♭, D♭, E, and G, can be combined to contain all the notes of a B, D, F, or A♭ diminished scale (they are all the same scale). Take each color chord combination in turn and experiment with combining the 7ths. For example, mix a D♭7 with a G7; and a B♭7 with an E7. Try all combinations of this color group as chords and arpeggios. Try playing two notes from, let's say, a B♭7, the A♭ and B♭ in the left hand and a G7 in the right hand as an arpeggio up the piano.

Here are some ideas to help you develop color chords:

1. When playing a ballad, add in color combinations whenever you have a dominant chord. You can also play with color chords as substitutions. Note that one of the color chord combinations is the tritone substitution. This is also a good modulation device.

2. It is also possible to think in terms of color chords when you are soloing. This works great when you are playing over any dominant or diminished chord. Keep in mind that a lot of the passing chords that you can use to move between one chord and another can be a diminished chord. This opens up fresh possibilities.

3. Practice the diminished exercise in all keys. (See example 8-11)

    1.   Bb Db E   G
    2.   B   D   F   Ab
    3.   C   Eb Gb A

Example 8-7: color chord combinations

Example 8-8: half/whole and whole/half diminished scales

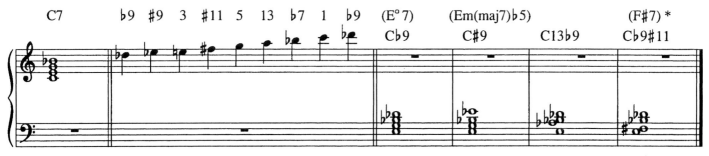

Example 8-9 diminished scale and chords

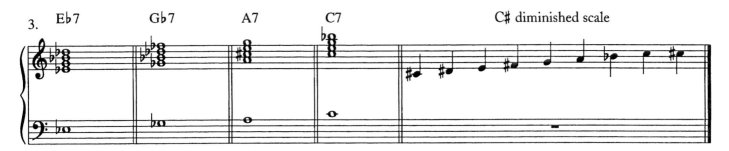

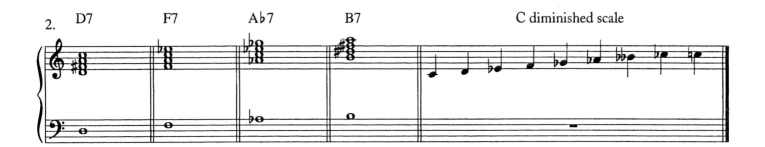

Example 8-10: color chords and diminished scale

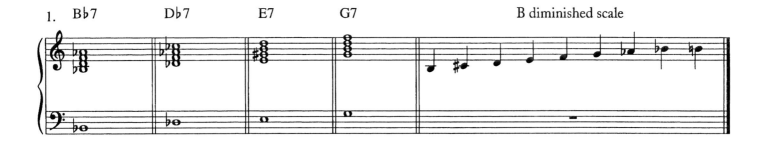

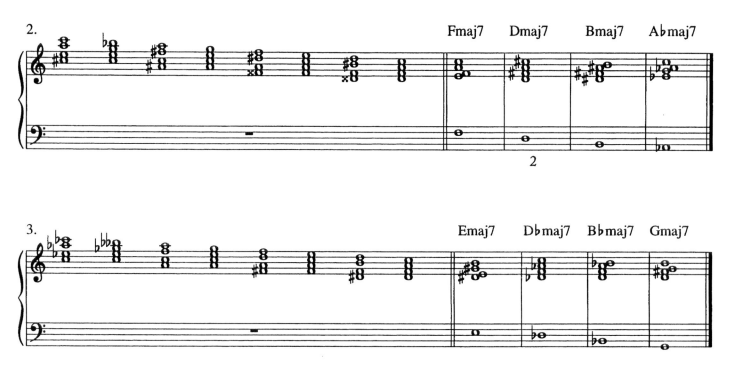

Example 8-11: diminished scale exercise

Learning New Voicings

In the area of jazz blues there are some specific voicings which will help you sound professional. Some of these are given below. A method is presented here to help you to assimilate these voicings, as well as other voicings you discover yourself.

I feel that it is more important to know how to find and assimilate your own voicings than to have someone tell you supposed hip voicings. Because if you have certain voicings which are elevated above others in importance, you, most assuredly, will use them over and over. In other words, you will probably sound like everyone else.

I like the idea of finding a sound, call it a chord or voicing first, then finding a purpose for it later. In other words, it is fun to sit at the piano, let your hands find a chordal sound that you like. Then you have to analyze it in terms of its intervalic content. Here is an example: The following chord or voicing is a sound commonly found in jazz. Some players call it the "So What" chord because it is used in a jazz tune by the same name. Just look at the chord, do not worry about its name or function. At this point, do not try to figure out its root. Just analyze the chord as an intervallic structure. In this case, it stacks two perfect fourths and a third on top. Let's call it 4-4-4-3. (See example 8-12)

Example 8-12: 4-4-4-3 voicing (so what chord)

Let's start by playing this voicing up and down chromatically. Think of it in its intervals. Let it float, do not worry about it's root. Then, play this voicing all over the piano, from very low to very high. Certainly, you will like some sounds, and others will not be pleasant to you. The main idea is to experience this particular sound.

Then start playing melodies using only this voicing. Even a simple nursery rhyme will do. (See Example 8-14) Play the voicing in many melodies and in all keys of the original melody. Try playing up a major scale with this voicing. The top note of the voicing plays the major scale. (See example 8-15)

It has been my observation that if you play a voicing enough times and in enough ways, it will find its way into your piano stylings. The subconscious will automatically start using it as part of your language. If you hear Chick Corea or Keith Jarrett play harmonies which you do not understand, remember that those harmonies are understandable to their subconscious. That is why they are able to use those harmonic structures so freely.

After you have familiarized yourself with the voicing, then you might want to analyze it in terms of the possible scales or modes that it belongs to and what possible roots can be played with it. In the case of quartal harmony, the harmonic structure is usually vague and many roots can be applied to it. The "So What" voicing can sound well in a major scale context; a Mixolydian mode context; or a minor context. It's a handy chord to use for comping. In general, it is a more modern sound to us than tertial harmony (chords in thirds).

Here are some commonly used jazz and blues voicings. (See example 8-13) Notice that some use perfect fourth intervals and some use the tritone or augmented fourth. It is recommended that you learn just one chord at a time. Of course, find your own chords and learn them. I have deliberately not included the roots. Play up the chromatic scale and you will find the roots which work.

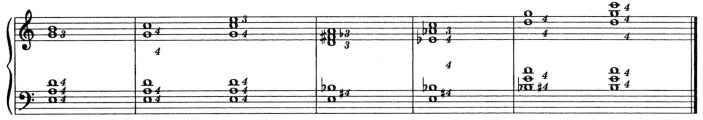

Example 8-13: some voicings

"So What" Chord 4-4-4-3

Example 8-14: melody harmonized with one voicing

Example 8-15: major scale played with one voicing

Scales for Jazz Blues Style

As said before, it is beyond the scope of this book to delve too deeply into jazz soloing. However, here are some scales for you to practice for jazz and advanced blues soloing:

1. Major scale and modes (See example 1-4)

2. Whole tone scales (See example 8-18)

3. Melodic minor and its modes. (See example 8-19)

4. Diminished scales (See example 8-8)

5. The blues scale

6. The altered scale (See example 8-16)

7. Pentatonics

Example 8-16: the altered scale

This scale for soloing is very effective when you have the interval of the ♯5 or, also known as the ♭13th. The chord sounds augmented. The altered chord is spelled with a ♭9 and a ♭13. Also, this chord is the seventh mode of the melodic scale. Experiment with this scale. This scale is effective with a dominant chord with an augmented 5th (flat 13), flat 9 or sharp 9, (and no major seventh)

Blues Scale - not to be used with major 7

Mixolydian Mode 5 - 5 of the Major Scale - not to be used with the major 7

Mixolydian + Mode (Notice the flat 3, 5, and 7) - no major 7

Diminished Scale - Whole Step / Half Step - no major 7 or flat 13

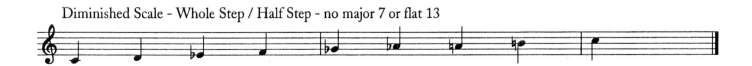

Altered Scale - 7 - 7 of the Melodic Minor Scale - no major 7

Example 8-17: some possible scales for blues soloing

C whole tone scale

Db whole tone scale

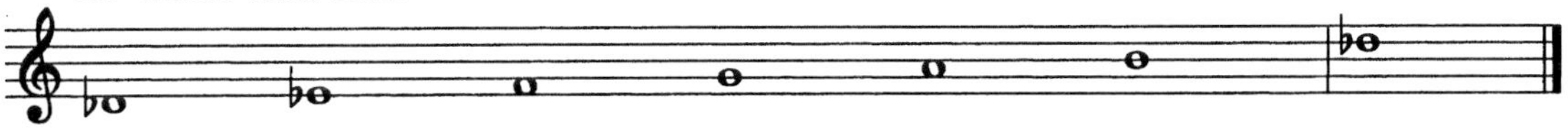

Example 8-18: whole tone scales

(1-1) melodic minor Cm(maj7)

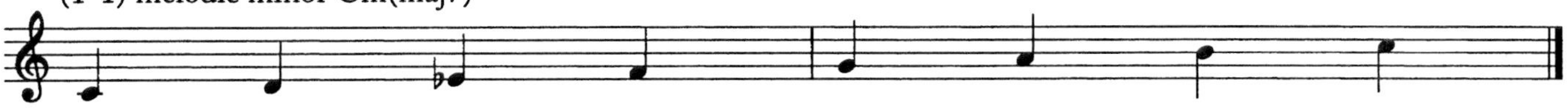

(2-2) Dorian b2 Cb9 C#9 Cm7

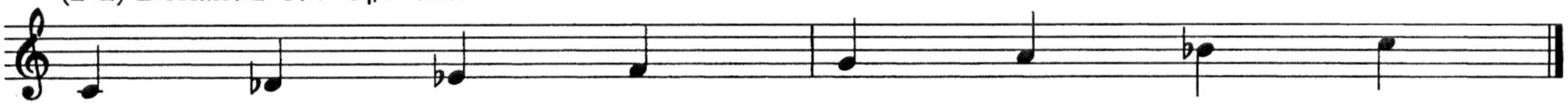

(3-3) Lydian augmented Cmaj7+

(4-4) Lydian b7 C#11 C13

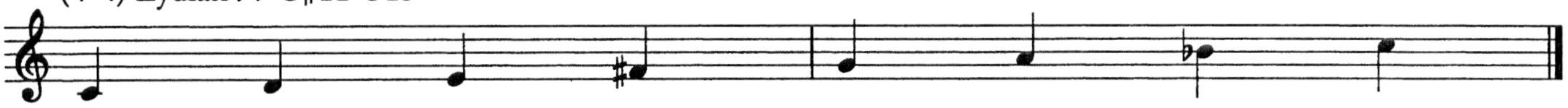

(5-5) Mixolydian b6 Cb13 C7+

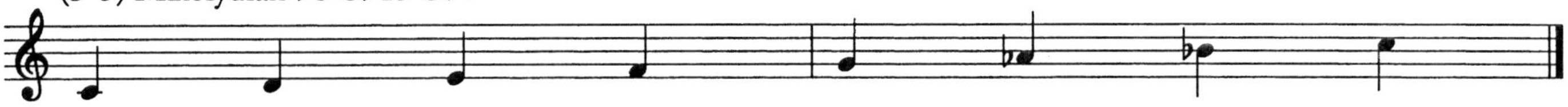

(6-6) Locrian #2 Cm7b5

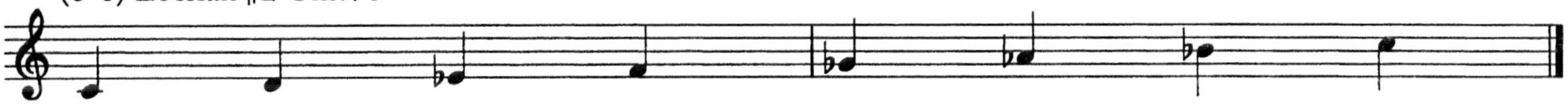

(7-7) Super Locrian (altered scale) Cb9b13 C#9b13

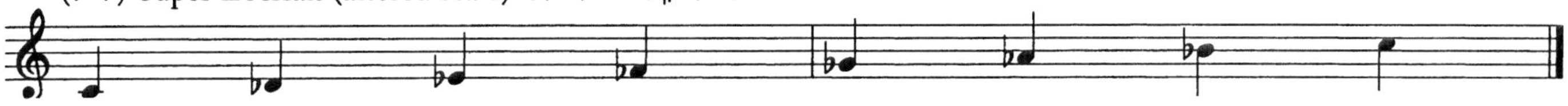

Example 8-19: melodic minor scales

Study each of the modes of the melodic minor scale. Notice the chords listed for each of the modes. You may solo over those chords with the respective modes.

Example 8-20: some pentatonics

Blues Forms

Here are just a few of the many, many blues forms. I have included a few hints for you to study. Consider all chords as including a flatted seventh, except the major seventh chords. Develop these changes until you can play them without thought. Learn them in all keys.

Basic Blues

C				F		C		G	F	C	G
1	2	3	4	5	6	7	8	9	10	11	12

Basic Blues with some alterations. Notice the II-V-I and diminished, half step above.

| C | F | C | Gm C | F | F#° | C | A | D | G | C A | D | G |

Gospel Blues - notice the use of the third in bass and diminished, half step above.

| C | C7/E | F F#° C/G | Gm7 C | F | F#° | C/G E/G# | A | D | G | C C/E F F#° C/G Ab | G |

Jazz be-bop changes - many uses of II-Vs and Tritone Substitution.

| C | F | Bm7b5 E | Am D | Gm C | F | Fm Bb | Em A | Ebm Ab | Dm | G | Em Eb | Dm Db |

More Jazz be-bop changes - many use of II-Vs and Tritone Substitution.

| Cmaj7 | Bm Bbm | Am Abm Gm Gbm | Fmaj7 | Fm | Em | Ebm | Dm | G | Dm G Em Ebm Dm Db |

More Jazz be-bop changes - Unusual use of Major Seventh. Lots of Tri-tone Subs.

| C | Bm E | Am D | Gm C | F | Fm Bb | Dm | Ebm A | Dm | G | Bb Eb | Ab | Db |

Basic Minor Blues - notice the II chord with flatted 5th. Notice the A7 altered chord.

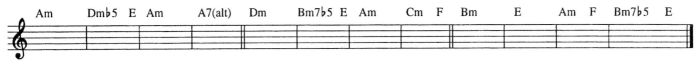

Example 8-21: some blues forms

Developing the Jazz Blues Style

After you have begun your development of jazz theory, then proceed to developing the jazz blues.

1. Pick a blues progression (blues form) that you would like to learn, by playing a single note in the left hand and a comping chord in the right hand. Don't forget to count out loud. (See example 8-21 and 8-22)

2. This should develop into a walking bass in the left hand and a chord in the right hand. (See example 8-25)

   In creating a walking bassline (and also, for soloing in general), first establish "target notes" in your mind. Usually the target notes will outline the chord changes of the tune. Notice that there are many ways to arrive at a target note. You can approach it from above or below, diatonically (by scales) or chromatically. (See example 8-23)

   Notice the little hops which looks like grace notes on the music. These are better explained by having you listen to bass players play walking basslines. They often propel the music forward by a slight hop. It is played lightly and quickly, and not in a melodic, but a rhythmical manner. They are automatically put in at the discretion of the bassist.

   The main emphasis is to play the basslines the way a bass player would approach them. Be aware of the groove that the bass player takes on different tunes. In the case of straight ahead blues jazz, he probably climbs on, or pushes the beat. This creates an aggressive, "cooking" groove. You have to spend a lot of practice time to create good, bass-player-like, walking basslines. Keep at it.

3. Then practice playing single notes in half notes or whole notes in the left hand and soloing in the right hand.

4. Then practice with left hand comping chords and right hand soloing. (See example 8-25) Use these chords for left hand comping.

5. Finally, and only when you are ready…play a walking bass in left hand and solo in the right hand. Listen to the CD for examples of the above exercise. (CD) (See example 8-23)

"Blues for Clark"

Here are some blues chord changes, chords, voicings, and some melodic sequences, and for the tune, "Blues for Clark." Listen to the phrasing of the sax, bass, and drums as well as the piano. Learn the basic chord changes. Then sit-in with the band.

By Martan Mann

Example 8-22: Blues for Clark chord changes

Example 8-23: Blues for Clark walking bassline

by Martan Mann

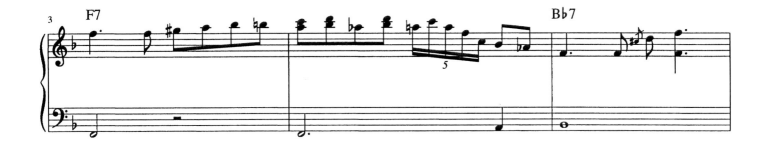

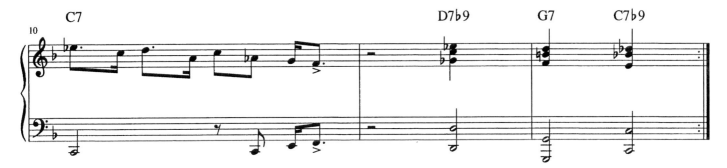

Example 8-24: Blues for Clark (single note in the bass, melody in the right hand)

Example 8-25: Blues for Clark (walking bassline and comping chords)

Chapter 9
Minor Blues Style

The minor blues style is very similar to the jazz blues style (in major) except that the form uses minor chord changes. Also practice the minor blues in the same routine as the jazz blues style. Here are a few of the differences to be aware of:

1. The II-V-Is are often a IIm9♭5, V7♭9, and Im9. For variations, (See exercise 9-1) Practice the II-V-I exercise around the cycle of 4ths, 5ths, and up and down chromatically.

2. You can still use the blues scale and the Mixolydian+ mode (heavy use of the minor third). However, you can also use the Dorian mode, melodic minor, natural minor, and harmonic minor scales and diminished scales.

3. Endings will be in minor. (See exercise 9-5)

4. The turnaround will often be a Im9, VI7♯9, II7♯9, V7♯9. (See exercise 9-6)

Developing the Minor Blues Style

Pick a minor blues progression that you would like to learn by playing a single note in the left hand and a chord in the right hand. The minor blues example on the CD is entitled, "formation." (See exercise 9-2)

1. This should develop into a walking bass in the left hand and a chord in the right hand. (See exercise 9-4)

2. Then practice playing single notes in half notes or whole notes in the left hand and soloing in the right hand.

3. Then practice with left hand chords and right hand soloing.

4. Finally, and only when you are ready...play a walking bass in left hand and solo in the right hand. (See exercise 9-4)

Example 9-1: basic II V I progression in minor

By Martan Mann

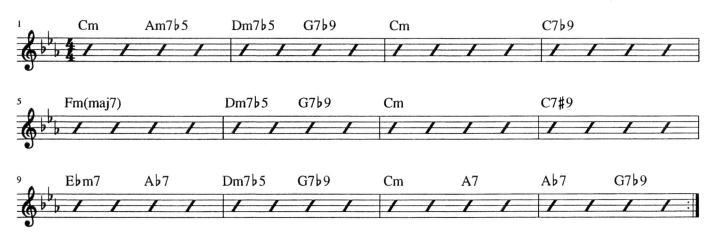

Example 9-2: Formation chord changes

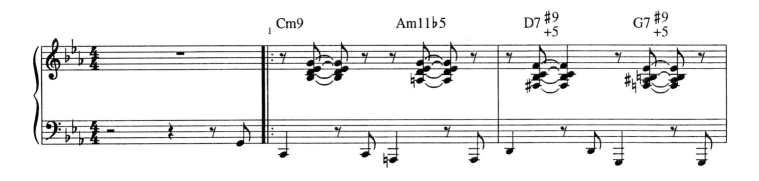

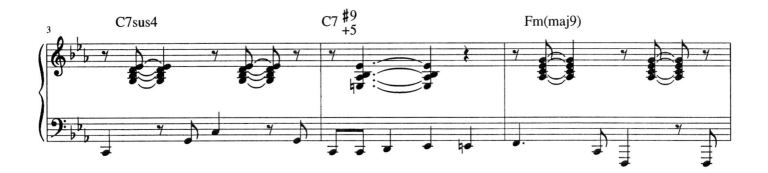

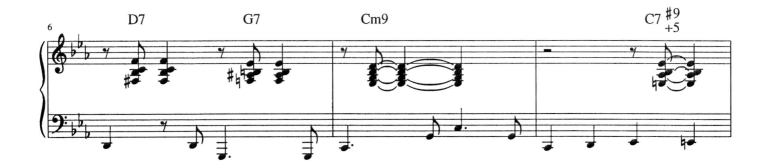

Example 9-3: Formation (half-time bass lines and comping chords)

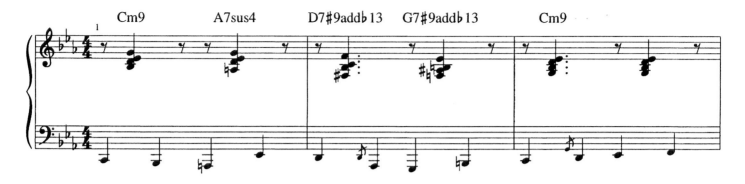

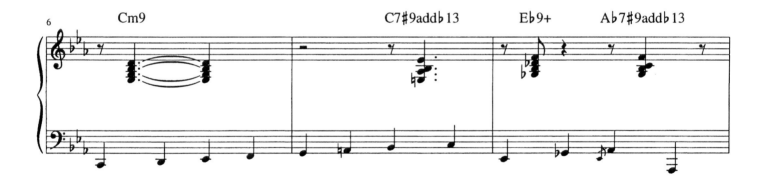

Example 9–4: Formation (walking bass line and comping chords in right hand)

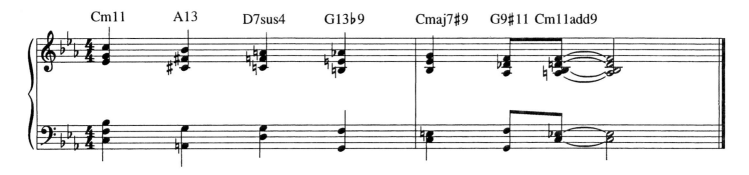

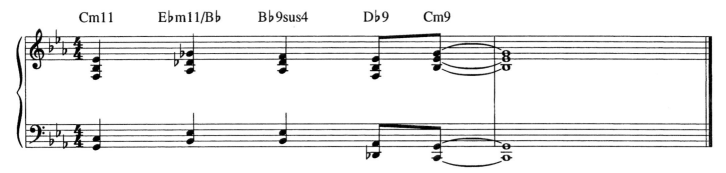

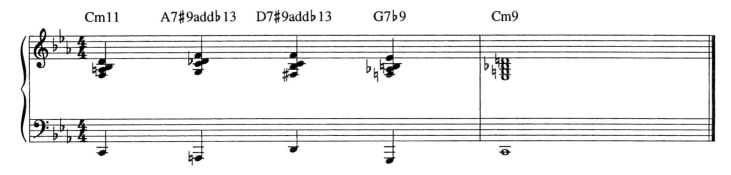

Example 9-5: some sample endings in minor

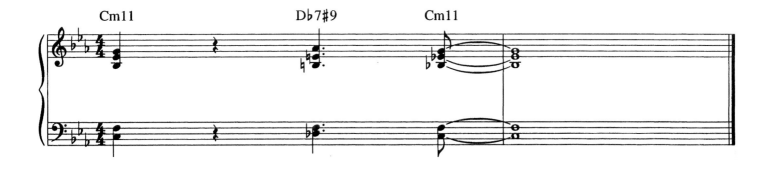

Example 9-6: sample minor turnaround

CD Track List

Chapter 1
Basic Theory
1. Learning the Dominant Seventh chord using the "Think Before Moving Exercise."
    a) Think Before Moving Exercise
    b) Example 1-12 - Dominant Seventh

Chapter 2
Boogie Woogie Style
2. Talking about the Basic 12-Bar Blues Pattern.
    a) Discussion of the Basic Blues Form
    b) Example 2-2 - Basic 12-Bar Blues Progression
3. Blues Scale(s)
    a) Discussion of the Blues Scale and Mixolydian Mode
    b) Example 2-12 - Dominant Seventh Chord
    c) Examples 2-3 and 2-4 - Mixolydian Mode and Blues Scale
4. Developing the Boogie Woogie Style
    a) Discussion of Developing the Boogie Woogie Style
    b) Example 2-6 - Basic Boogie Woogie Blues
    c) Discussion of the "Groove"
    d) Example 2-6 - Basic Boogie Woogie Blues (for Groove)
    e) Example 2-7 & 2-8 - Boogie Woogie with Rhythmic Patterns
    f) Advice on Soloing
    g) Example 2-13 - Soloing Melody to One Note ("F")
    h) Example 2-14 - Soloing Using Repeating Ideas
    i) Example 2-9 - Boogie Woogie Blues Lick
       Alternating between thumb and other fingers
5. Boogie Woogie Blues sung by Charmaigne Scott
    a) Discussion of CD Performance
    b) Example 2-15 - Boogie Woogie Chord Changes
    c) Example 2-16 - CD Blues Licks

Chapter 3
Tritone Blues Style
6. Introduction of the Tritone Style
    a) Example 3-1 - Tritone Blues Chord Changes
7. Development of the Tritone Blues
    a) Discussion of Development of the Tritone Blues Style
    b) Example 3-2 - Tritone Blues
       Left Hand Bass, Right Hand Ostinato
    c) Example 3-3 - Tritone Blues
       Tritone in Left Hand, Rhythmic Figures in Right Hand
    d) Example 3-4 - Tritone Blues
       Single Note in the Left Hand, Soloing in the Right Hand
    e) Example 3-5 - Tritone Blues
       Tritone in the Left Hand, Soloing in the Right Hand

b) Example 6-2 - Funk Rhythm
   with Single Note in Bass and Chord Structures in Right Hand
c) Example 6-4 - "Santa Cruz Funk" Lead-ins in the Bass

Chapter 7
Rock Blues Style

19. Introduction of the Rock Blues Style
    a) Discussion of the Rock Blues Style
20. Development of the Rock Blues Style
    a) Example 7-1 - Blues Rock Accompaniment
    b) Example 7-2 - Some Blues Rock Licks
    c) Example 7-3 - Some Blues Rock Endings

Chapter 8
Jazz Blues Style

21. Introduction of the Jazz Blues Style
    a) Discussion of the Jazz Blues Style
22. Development of the Jazz Blues Theory
    a) Example 8-1 & 8-2 - Basic II-V-I Progression in Major
    b) Example 8-3 - Chord in Left Hand without the Root Note
    c) Example 8-4 - II-V-I-VI Left Hand Single Bass Note - Right
       Hand Chords
    d) Example 8-16 - Altered Scale
    e) Example 8-19 - Melodic Minor Scale
    f) Example 8-6
       Some Possible Alterations of the II, V, and I Chords
    g) Example 8-17 - Scales for Jazz Blues Soloing
    h) Example 8-5 - II-V-I-VI
       Left Hand Walking Basslines - Right Hand Chords or Soloing
    i) Discussion of Diminished Scales
    j) Example 8-8 - Diminished Scales
    k) Example 8-20 - Some Blues Forms
23. Development of Jazz Blues Style ("Blues for Clark")
    a) Discussion of Developing the Jazz Blues Style
    b) Example 8-21 - "Blues for Clark"
       Chord Changes for Jazz Blues
    c) Example 8-24 - "Blues for Clark"
       Walking Bass and Comping Chords
       (Use this accompaniment to practice soloing)
    d) Example 8-22 - "Blues for Clark"
       Single notes in the Left Hand, Soloing in the Right Hand
    e) Example 8-22 - "Blues for Clark"
       Walking Bass in Left Hand, Soloing in the Right Hand
    f) Example 8-23 - "Blues for Clark"
       Single Note in the Bass/Melody in Right Hand

Chapter 9
Minor Blues Style

24. Introduction of the Minor Blues Style
    a) Discussion of the Minor Blues Style
25. Development of the Minor Blues Theory
    a) Example 9-1 - II-V-I Progression in Minor
    b) Example 9-5 - Some Sample Endings in Minor
    c) Example 9-6 - Minor Turnaround
26. Development of Minor Blues Style ("Formation")
    a) Example 9-1 - "Formation" Chord Changes
    b) Example 9-3 - "Formation"
       Half-Time Basslines and Comping Chords
    c) Example 9-4 - "Formation"
       Walking Basslines and Comping Chords in Right Hand